HF
5415.13
.T39
1994

Teagno, Gary C.

Profiting through
association
marketing.

$35.00

DATE			

BAKER & TAYLOR

PROFITING THROUGH ASSOCIATION MARKETING

PROFITING THROUGH ASSOCIATION MARKETING

Gary C. Teagno

IRWIN
Professional Publishing
Burr Ridge, Illinois
New York, New York

© RICHARD D. IRWIN, INC., 1994

Editor: Carol Rogala
Project editor: Lynne Basler
Production manager: Ann Cassady
Designer: Mercedes Santos
Art coordinator: Heather Burbridge
Compositor: Wm. C. Brown Communications, Inc.
Typeface: 11/13 Palatino
Printer: R. R. Donnelley & Sons Company

Library of Congress Cataloging-in-Publication Data

Teagno, Gary C.
  Profiting through association marketing/Gary C. Teagno.
    p.   cm.
  Includes index.
  ISBN 1–55623–836–3
  1. Marketing—United States—Planning.   2. Trade and professional Associations—United States—Management.
  HF5415.13.T39   1994
  658.8—dc20   93–14387

Printed in the United States of America
1 2 3 4 5 6 7 8 9 0 DOC 0 9 8 7 6 5 4 3

To
Ken Guenther,
my mentor,
and to
Pam, Kari, and Jeffrey,
my inspiration

Preface

Profiting through Association Marketing was developed to provide an insider's look at the 100,000 associations thriving in America and show how they can assist corporations to garner market share. Each association represents a readymade target market of motivated prospects. For the members of each association share a common bond—whatever their occupations, vocations, or preoccupations. Association members highly regard the association that has earned their dues, and they support its programs.

We will examine the association market; its motivations, decision making, and "hot-buttons." The book also details the opportunities for program development, association prospecting, the close, and successful member marketing.

The challenge is to select the association that best represents your customers or prospects, and design programs that meet the associations's needs. Our goal is to help locate your ideal association and build a program that is too good to refuse.

ACKNOWLEDGMENTS

This book would not have been possible without the encouragement and support of the American Society of Association Executives (ASAE) and the dedicated staff of the ASAE's Information Central. While many at the association contributed to the effort, special thanks to ASAE President R. William Taylor and to the boundless energy and enthusiasm of ASAE's vice president of Publishing Elissa Myers.

Many other companies and associations also contributed by sharing their experiences, successes and hurdles:

Acropolis Books Ltd.
AFLAC Inc.
Air Conditioning Contractors of America
American Association of Retired Persons
American Institute of Certified Public Accountants
American Physical Therapy Association
American Society of Association Executives
American Trucking Associations
AON Specialty Group
Automotive Service Industry Association
Avis Rental Car System
Camelot Travel Services
Chicago Society of Association Executives
Commercial Life Insurance Company
Distributive Education Clubs of America
The Equitable Life Assurance Society
French & Associates, Inc.
Healthcare Financial Management Association
Independent Bankers Association of America
Lawrence-Leiter and Company
Legg Mason Wood Walker, Inc.
Meridian One Corporation
National Association of College Stores
National Association of Realtors®
Penny-Wise Office Products
PHH U.S. Mortgage Corporation
Pitney Bowes
Produce Marketing Association
The Prudential
Royal Insurance
The St. Paul Companies
Schlegel & Associates
Society of National Association Publications
Trade Show Bureau
United Airlines Inc.
U.S. Sprint
Visa International
Washington Resource Consulting Group
Xerox Corporation

The author also wishes to acknowledge Leonard J. Rubin of Bracewell & Patterson and Joseph Greif of McNeily & Rosenfeld for their assistance in Chapter 12, The Agreement.

Gary C. Teagno

Contents

Chapter One

A Nation of Associations

Americans of all ages, all stations of life, and all types of dispositions are forever forming associations. They have not only commercial and industrial associations in which all take part, but others of a thousand different types—religious, moral, serious, futile, very general and very limited, immensely large and very minute.[1]

America is indeed a nation of associations. The IRS estimates that there are now over one million tax-exempt organizations in the United States. Michael O'Neill, the author of *The Third America*, states that this sector of America "owns 10 percent of the nation's property, employs as many civilians as the federal and state government combined, has a bigger budget than all but seven nations in the world."[2] While the nonprofit sector includes such diverse groups as charities, churches, schools, hospitals, and museums, only one group of nonprofits is dedicated to representing the interests of individuals and businesses across the nation: associations.

While associations can be traced back to the ancient cultures of Rome and the Orient, the growth of associations as we know them today began in the Middle Ages with the guilds that were established to protect the interests of merchants and their families. While the Industrial Revolution diminished the importance of medieval guilds, the growth of associations in America was just beginning in the 18th century, witnessed by the rapid growth of cooperative trade groups and chambers of commerce formed to promote favorable business conditions. With the advent of the Civil War and the nation's subsequent industrialization,

1

association and chamber of commerce formation accelerated to meet the growth of specialized industry. Many of the associations formed in the 1800s continue to serve members today:[3]

American Statistical Association (1839)

American Psychiatric Association (1844)

American Medical Association (1847)

American Pharmaceutical Association (1852)

American Iron and Steel Institute (1855)

National Education Association (1857)

American Dental Association (1859)

At the beginning of the 20th century, only 100 national associations existed in the United States, but by the end of World War I, in order to meet the nation's tremendous industrial demands, over 1,000 national associations had been established.[4] To foster economic development and export trade, the number of national associations doubled, to approximately 2,000 following the Depression and World War II.

Spawned by the increasing specialization of industry and the birth of new technologies, the number of national associations continued to grow at a steady pace, reaching 5,000 in 1956 and 13,000 in 1975. In the last 25 years, because of the continued economic growth of the nation, the number of associations has quadrupled to meet the needs of both individuals and businesses.[5]

The enormous influence of associations affects every American. A recent study by the American Society of Association Executives (ASAE) and the ASAE Foundation found that 7 out of 10 Americans belong to at least one association, and 4 out of 10 belong to four or more. Just the top 200 associations in the United States represent over 260,000,000 members—more than the population of the United States.[6]

The top dozen associations, ranked by membership, are virtually household names:*

---

*Source: *Association Fact Book*, published by the American Society of Association Executives.

American Association of Retired Persons

American Automobile Association

YMCA of the USA

National Geographic Society

National PTA

National Wildlife Federation

Boy Scouts of America

4-H Programs

Girl Scouts of the USA

American Heart Association

American Legion

National Rifle Association

Contrary to what most people believe, associations are not principally "political animals." According to research conducted by the Hudson Institute for the American Society of Association Executives, the major roles of associations are:

1. Setting, certifying, and meeting product standards. Voluntary standards, established by an association are generally preferred over government regulations because they are often more flexible and adaptable and they help ensure the compatibility and interchangability of products and parts. In 1990, the association members surveyed spent $14.5 billion to meet voluntary rules.

2. Education—almost 90 percent of associations surveyed offer educational programs to their members and disseminate information to the public. Through their educational offerings, associations translate general information into concrete practices in industry and professions, provide technical education assistance and management training.

3. Encouraging professional conduct through the establishment of standards, certification, accreditation, and licensing. While secondary education, graduate training, and state licensing form the basis, associations promote professional conduct through peer review, courses that meet legal requirements, and the issuing of standards that often form the basis of disciplinary action.

4. Information—almost 65 percent of associations gather statistics and facilitate or conduct research. Many institutions, including the government, depend on associations for statistical information, on which to base policy debate.

5. Political representation. Overall, associations spend less than
   10 percent of total annual expenses on political education,
   often concentrating on explaining new regulations and
   guidelines, rather than lobbying. Associations also provide
   information to Congress and other government agencies on the
   potential effect of proposed legislation or regulations on their
   members.[7]

Over 100,000 associations now exist at the national, state, and
local levels. These associations vary in nature as widely as the
occupations, vocations, and preoccupations of Americans. For
almost every cause, belief, or position there are likely to be associations that represent its proponents and associations that
represent its opponents. The common bonds that association
members share are marketing dreams come true, for not only do
members share common traits, but they believe in their association and in the programs it supports.

The essence of target marketing is getting your message in
front of motivated prospects. Because the average sales call now
costs $275 and the average sale takes 5.5 sales calls, target mar-
keting is an economic necessity.[8] Through target marketing,
return on investment is improved through the elimination of un-
productive promotional, advertising, sales, and marketing
efforts.

David Cravens, in his book *Strategic Marketing*, states, "When
you analyze the corporate and marketing strategies of successful
companies, one feature stands out. Each has a target market
strategy that has proven to be a major factor in gaining a strong
market position for the firm, although the actual strategies used
by firms and the business units within them are often quite
different."[9]

In traditional target marketing, the sales process usually
begins with a corporate examination of current customers and
prospects to determine the factors that the groups have in
common. For individuals, depending on the product, you might
examine income, location, purchasing habits, purpose of the purchase, criteria for purchase, product features, occupations, and
even lifestyle. If your target is other businesses, you might examine the industry, the location, the application, and requirements and service needs.

Once you've defined the target market, you have to determine if and how it can be reached. An effective marketing strategy will likely involve utilizing the expertise of list brokers to target direct mail and using advertising agencies to focus media exposure. Through the traditional process of establishing a target market, you have established a de facto "association" of people or businesses that share common characteristics and buying habits.

Traditional target markets are composed of businesses or individuals who are unaware of their selection and lack any direct connection to anyone else in the same group or to those who established the group. Members of an association, however, have an established affinity with the association. That sense of affinity is a strong motivator since the decision to buy is often influenced by the actions of peers, the "seal of approval" of a trusted party, or the confidence that a supplier understands the buyer's needs.

ASSOCIATION ACCESS

Associations are target markets, for each association is comprised of individuals or businesses that share common characteristics and buying patterns. Associations are a cut above fabricated target markets because the members of associations not only share a common bond, but belong to an established group of their peers and have expressed their ongoing support of the group through participation and the payment of dues.

There are two methods to access a target market through an association. The first option, traditional association marketing, involves taking an active role within the association that represents your customers and prospects. This approach permits your advertising, promotion, and marketing to be targeted, increasing its relevancy and effectiveness. The second approach is to market in partnership with associations. Association partnerships permit you to leverage your product expertise and marketing with the name, goodwill, and access to the association. Unlike traditional association marketing, partnerships provide an unparalleled opportunity to target market with the "seal of approval" of an association that has earned the respect of its members.

Depending on the product, its marketing, sales force, and support, each association marketing option offers significant target-marketing potential.

Traditional Association Marketing

Most associations provide companies opportunities to reach their membership. While access to membership differs in each association, all can provide a conduit to target your marketing to an audience comprised of your current buyers or prospects. Associations offer traditional advertising and marketing support as well as methods unique to associations:

Association advertising. Almost all associations publish magazines or newsletters, and the majority accept advertising. One of the reasons association advertising is often overlooked is that most associations do not employ sales representatives, and their publications may not have the mass circulation that attracts corporations or their advertising agencies. However, association publications score very well in readership surveys due to the intimacy between the members and the publication. For advertisers high readership is the bottom line.[10]

Don't overlook the potential of garnering free publicity for your company and its products since many association magazines publish corporate announcements about new products or services of interest to their members. In addition, association magazines are often on the lookout for new articles or fresh approaches to an industry problem. Take the time to talk with the editor and submit articles that provide useful information, not just corporate promotion.

Mailing lists. Many associations sell or rent lists of their membership. These lists are kept current since they are based on the association's membership billings. To limit any chance that the association's name or endorsement is used or implied, associations will usually review all membership mailings or conduct the mailing on behalf of the vendor. Some associations will restrict the usage of membership lists to vendors that have an established relationship with the association or who are members of the association.

Convention/Trade shows. Most associations have annual conventions and trade shows that represent excellent opportunities to showcase your products or services. Since many trade shows attract more than 10 percent of an association's membership, they are a cost effective alternative to one-on-one sales calls. Generally, convention attendance and exhibition-booth rental are available to all interested companies. However, vendors who have an established relationship with the association often receive preferred site selection and early notification.

Although exhibiting is the most frequent convention activity, other opportunities may exist. Explore association interest in your sponsorship of a seminar scheduled during or preceding the convention. These sessions can be excellent forums both to display your expertise and to introduce products and personnel. Other convention options include the hosting of a hospitality suite to welcome users and prospects or the sponsorship of a convention event, such as a meal function or reception.

Scholarships/Capital campaigns. Associations may offer other opportunities for you to demonstrate your company's commitment to the association and its membership. Association foundations often seek corporate sponsors for industry research, scholarships, or educational programs. Associations may also seek project financing and conduct capital campaigns for specific studies and long-term financing. These fund drives are opportunities for corporations to provide tangible evidence of their industry support.

Membership. Approximately 50 percent of associations permit suppliers to become association members, usually called associate or affiliate members.[11] Generally, associate membership provides corporations with increased visibility among the membership and grants the corporation certain access unavailable to nonassociate members.

The most common associate benefits include subscriptions to, and advertising discounts in, association magazines, advance notice of trade shows, discounts on booth-rental fees, and access to association educational seminars. It is interesting to note that one-third of associations even permit associate members to hold office.

Before you conclude that associate membership is too good to be true, let's examine its limitations. Associations are very careful not to convey the idea that associate membership implies endorsement of any vendor or any specific product. Therefore, most associations expressly prohibit associate members from advertising their associate membership, utilizing the association's logo or name, or implying the association's endorsement of the associate member's products or services in their marketing and advertising. Such prohibitions are designed to avoid confusing the membership and to retain the value of the association's endorsement.

While most associations provide opportunities for companies to market to their membership, this access is carefully monitored to ensure that the association is not seen as endorsing the corporation or its products. Some companies, however, have discovered a method to access the association's membership and market with the "seal of approval" of the association.

Association Partnerships

Association partnerships provide companies access to a target market and the ability to market with the "seal of approval" of the association that has earned the respect of its members. The endorsement of an association can help increase market share, cement industry dominance, or provide access to a new market. Marketing through an association provides a method to "brand" your product and differentiate it from others. In an association-sponsored program, your product or service is branded with the association's name and logo and therefore its goodwill, distinguishing it from others in the market. Such branding, when combined with exclusive access to the membership, can provide a significant marketing edge, shortening evaluation time and encouraging members to buy with confidence.

James Rosenfield, author of *Financial Services Direct Marketing*, states that "strong brands provide control, comfort, and confidence. They also, importantly, offer an antidote to complexity: A brand is a simplification tool. Brand loyalty streamlines the decision-making process: 'This is my brand, I trust it, I'll use it, and thankfully eliminate a decision from the thousands of choices I have to make each day.' "[12]

Marketing through nonprofits, including associations, is not new. Affinity programs, as they are often referred to, have been used to market products for well over 20 years. Affinity marketing relies on the strong "seal of approval" or brand of the association to increase sales and usage over products that lack such affinity or brand. We have all experienced the impact of affinity marketing. Witness the success of Girl Scout Cookies or the widespread usage of affinity credit cards that bear the name and logo of associations across America that now represent over 10 percent of all credit cards.

More recently we have witnessed the growth of cause-related marketing that markets products or services with the affinity of a worthy cause or charity. Such marketing attempts to make a product stand for something that the consumer feels strongly about, in an effort to increase the consumers' positive view of the product and, ultimately, increase sales. In a recent survey conducted by the Counselors Academy of Public Relations Society of America, cause-related marketing ranked at the top of the list of the 10 hottest trends in the industry.[13]

According to the "Study of Cause-Related Marketing" conducted by Sheridan Associates and Zimmerman Associates and distributed by the Independent Sector, corporations view cause-related marketing as a sales approach that links the corporation's products with the good feelings of the cause. The corporation's objectives often include generating sales among consumers or businesses, impacting the company or brand image, assisting the cause, generating goodwill, and motivating sales forces and employees. The charity, on the other hand, according to the same study, was often seeking additional revenue in addition to its fund-raising and other activities, increased public awareness, recruitment of volunteers or supporters, the changing of public attitudes through the distribution of educational information, and the leveraging of corporate resources.[14]

The "Study of Cause-Related Marketing" found that "most corporations and charitable organizations surveyed are supportive of cause-related marketing, considering it appropriate and useful for their organizations. They view it as a win/win situation for the corporation, the cause and the consumer."[15]

Association partnerships can be just such a win-win situation, for a well-designed program can provide the corporate partner and the association five critical advantages:

1. *Increased Market Share.* Corporations gain the ability to target market their products and services, not simply to industries or professions but to occupations within industry sectors and specialties within professions. Such specific marketing permits companies to target buyers and prospects of both industry-wide and niche products, to further focus marketing, advertising, and sales efforts to increase market share. Association programs also provide a vendor the ability to "stake-out" the association's territory and make the entrance of new competition very difficult indeed, for through exposure within the association's activities, the company is viewed as an integral part of the association. With over 100,000 associations, there is an association that represents the prospects of virtually any product or service.

Associations are also seeking an increased market share. The market for associations, however, is not products or services, but membership. The lifeblood of any association is members, and well-designed service partnerships enable it both to attract and to retain members. The greater the association's membership, the greater its ability to meet its membership's needs.

2. *Marketing Leverage.* Association partnerships offer the corporate partner the ability to leverage their advertising, sales force, and promotional efforts with the membership clout and exclusive marketing and communication channels of the association. Such exclusive access provides a marketing forum without parity when combined with corporate promotional and advertising resources. For associations provide access to members who share common goals and needs and are motivated both by the actions of their peers and by the credibility of the association.

Associations are also seeking to harness the marketing leverage of their corporate partners. Since most associations lack full-time marketing departments and generally rely on direct mail and volunteers for their recruitment activity, the marketing of the corporate partner often provides invaluable "piggy-back" marketing exposure for the association to promote the benefits of membership.

3. *Credibility.* An association program provides corporations with use of the association's "seal of approval." Association programs provide an opportunity to market products or services through the association's goodwill. Consumers are confronted with more options than ever before, and association programs enable members to simplify their decision making by relying on the evaluation of their peers and the association.

An association's credibility can also be enhanced through the provision of quality products and member services. Products and services that add to the value of membership enhance the association's image among its membership and broaden its appeal to membership prospects.

4. *Enhanced Visibility.* Associations offer many opportunities for corporations to increase their industry or professional visibility. Through trade shows, conventions, association publications, and member communication channels, a corporation and its products gain an increased awareness among its targeted audience. When an association promotes association membership and the services that membership includes, its partner gains invaluable visibility that can also save marketing and advertising costs.

Associations also seek increased visibility and awareness. While most associations do not have the resources to mass market to the general public or personally call on members and nonmembers, corporate partnerships often provide an alternative vehicle. For each time that a corporation promotes the service or program, the association's name is broadcast, and each time the company's sales force calls on association prospects, the association's visibility is increased.

5. *Product Development.* An association partnership permits a company to better understand the needs of the members. Through networking and association research, companies are able to develop products tailored to the needs of the membership, which, in turn, generates additional partnership opportunities.

Through partnerships, associations also gain the ability to develop new products and services. For while associations have research capability, they often lack the resources or expertise to exploit new ideas or implement new programs; corporate partnerships often enable associations to bring them to fruition. As the potential array of program delivery systems becomes increasingly technologically based, association dependence on corporate sponsors is bound to increase.

Understanding the association market and its unique organizational structure is critical to your success. The more targeted that your marketing becomes, the greater the odds of its success.

NOTES

1. Alexis de Tocqueville, *Democracy in America* (Vintage Books, 1954), vol. 1.
2. Michael O'Neil, *The Third America* (Jossey-Bass, 1989) pp. 1–2.
3. American Society of Association Executives, *Association Fact Book* (ASAE). p. 12.
4. Ibid., p. 17.
5. Ibid., p. 18.
6. Elissa Myers, "The 100 Largest," *Association Management* (May 1992), p. 10.
7. American Society of Association Executives, *Executive Summary of Associations Advance America* (ASAE, 1990), pp. 2–3.
8. Jay Conrad Levinson, *Guerrilla Marketing Attack* (Houghton Mifflin, 1989), p. 43.
9. David Cravens, *Strategic Marketing* (Richard D. Irwin, Inc., 1982).
10. Ron Bognore, "Professional and Trade Associations: Direct Connections to Your Markets," *Business Marketing* (September 1992), p. 4.
11. American Society of Association Executives, *Policies and Procedures in Association Management* (ASAE, 1992), p. 74.

12. James R. Rosenfield, *Financial Services Direct Marketing* (Financial Sourcebooks, 1991), pp. 4–7.

13. Don Oldenburg, "Socially Correct Marketing," *Washington Post* June 23, 1992.

14. Sheridan Associates and Zimmerman Associates, "Study of Cause-Related Marketing" (Independent Sector, 1988) pp. 7–8.

15. Ibid., p. 11.

Chapter Two

Association Target Marketing

From a marketing prospective it is critical to recognize that associations vary as widely as the memberships they represent. Associations, like their corporate counterparts, range from one-person offices to fully staffed operations with subsidiaries and affiliates. While some associations represent businesses, others represent individuals, and while one association's membership will number only a few in one state, other associations represent millions of members located internationally.

TRADE AND PROFESSIONAL ASSOCIATIONS

There are two different types of associations that represent two distinct groups of prospects. Associations that represent manufacturers, distributors, importers, retailers, contractors, and other businesses are referred to as *trade associations*. Trade associations are not-for-profit organizations usually composed of competitors who come together out of desire to improve their economic status.[1] Trade associations are, in a sense, nonprofit extensions of the for-profit world, often providing businesses information, education, and political representation that would be costly and largely impractical on an individual basis.[2]

Trade associations typically provide their members educational meetings and seminars to hone skills, industry-specific newsletters and publications, a conduit to influence regulation or legislation that may affect members, and the opportunity for businesses to share experiences and problems with others in their field. A survey conducted by the Foundation for Public Affairs found that corporations are increasingly leaning on their trade associations for federal government relations. The survey found that almost 84 percent of corporations rely on their association, 56 percent on their Washington-based office, and 38 percent utilize Washington-based law firms.

Barry R. Schimel, CPA, states in *100 Ways to Prosper in Today's Economy*, "No organization struggling through a rough economic period needs to face adversity alone. If your company is hurting, others in your industry are almost certainly feeling pain as well . . . trade associations can be a business lifeline in a sagging economy."[3]

While the average trade association represents 2,300 members, trade associations vary from those with only a dozen members, such as the Motor Vehicle Manufactures Association, to others with over 100,000 members:*

Independent Insurance Agents of American—280,000

United States Chamber of Commerce—219,000

National Association of Home Builders—160,000

National Apartment Association—35,000

National Automobile Dealers Association—19,000

National Funeral Directors Association—15,000

American Bonanza Society—10,200

Unlike trade associations, professional associations or individual membership societies represent individuals or professionals. Society members usually share common professions, interests, or objectives and are often composed of individuals who have acquired knowledge and experience that qualifies them as specialists; occasionally, membership in a professional association may be limited to those who have received specific professional credentials. The mission of professional societies commonly focuses on advocacy of the profession or interest group, encouraging high ethical standards and providing ongoing education and information.

---

*American Society of Association Executives. Used with permission.

Professional associations or societies range from broad-based groups, such as the American Association of Retired Persons and the American Automobile Association, to societies that represent specific vocations or professions, such as the American Chemical Society and the International Society of Stamp Collectors. The membership of professional societies varies accordingly; while the average society has 40,000 members, membership ranges from a few hundred to over 30 million:*

American Automobile Association—34,000,000

American Association of Retired Persons—32,700,000

National Right to Life Committee—12,000,000

American Farm Bureau Federation—4,100,000

National Education Association—2,150,000

National Association of Realtors—735,000

Ducks Unlimited—500,000

Boat Owners Association of the United States—450,000

NATIONAL, STATE, AND LOCAL ASSOCIATIONS

While many of the associations that are household names represent members nationwide or worldwide, the majority of associations are composed of members from only a city, state, or region (see Exhibit 2–1).

While some associations are totally independent, many are related, formally or informally, to other associations. The relationship between the national association and its state and local chapters and affiliates is important to understand, for it often influences the consideration, development, decision making, support, and marketing of services. It is not uncommon for a national association to have 50 state chapters that represent members in areas including state government and the delivery of educational

---

*American Society of Association Executives. Used with permission.

EXHIBIT 2–1
Associations by Scope

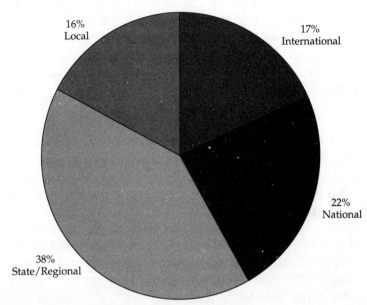

16%
Local

17%
International

22%
National

38%
State/Regional

Source: *Policies and Procedures in Association Management.* American Society of Association Executives, © 1992. Used with permission.

programs, as well as multiple local affiliates that may provide member support on a county or city level:*

National Association of REALTORS—50 state association chapters and 1,800 local boards of REALTORS.

American Medical Association—50 chapters and 2,000 local and regional affiliates.

American Library Association—57 library associations in states, regions, and territories of the United States.

Most associations with chapters or affiliates are organized in a federated structure, where members join an association, which

———

National Trade and Professional Associations of the U.S. Columbia Books, © 1993. Used with permission.

in turn joins another association. From the national perspective the advantages of such federated structures include a more effective means for obtaining grassroots input; benefits of local member recruitment and retention efforts; national leaders who have local and state experience and who enable better communication between local members and their national, state, and local associations; the perception of federated associations as grassroots organizations and therefore as more politically potent; and on-site assistance when conducting programs at the local level.[4]

On the other hand, national associations also point to the disadvantages of a federation: member loyalty usually rests with the local association, which can result in poor local communication of national issues; ego conflicts may occur between local and national leaders; the local association can financially control or manipulate the national association; occasional duplications, if not competition, of services and activities may occur; and major conflicts over public policy may stem from geographic differences at the local level.[5]

There are two major federated association structures. While in both scenarios the member pays dues to only one organization, which in turn funds the other association, each structure affects the relationship between the national association and its state or local affiliates in a slightly different way. About 44 percent of the time, membership in the national association includes membership in the local chapter.[6] Under this scenario, the member pays dues only to the national association, which includes membership in a local society or association. In this organizational structure, most activities, staff, and control reside at the national level, rather than at the local level. This structure is often common where a large national association decides to form chapters to facilitate communication and interaction with members locally.[7]

In 34 percent of associations, the member pays dues to the local chapter, which in turn funds the national association.[8] In this structure, the national association is often formed after chapters have become strong and see the advantages of forming a national coordinating body to help them communicate. Under this scenario, budget, staff size, activities, and therefore control and power, usually reside at the local level.[9]

In the majority of national associations with local affiliates, membership is dual; however, in approximately 19 percent of associations, members pay separate dues to the national and state associations and therefore can belong to one or both of the associations.[10] These organizations often have no overlap in governing structure, little coordination between the units, and often offer competing programs and services.[11]

Some larger associations also have regional offices that represent members locally. These offices are essentially branch offices of the parent association and usually do not impose separate dues. The regional offices, found in 12 percent of associations, often provide local assistance for government affairs, educational programs, and membership marketing and recruitment.[12]

The organization and relationship between an association and its chapters or affiliates is of critical importance to corporations seeking their marketing assistance. An association's relationship with its affiliates will often affect the association's marketing effectiveness, its desire to develop and offer new services, its decision-making process, and its role in attracting and retaining members.

ASSOCIATION SECTIONS AND COUNCILS

In response to the growing complexity and diversity of their members, about 25 percent of associations now have councils or sections comprised of members who share occupations or specialties.[13] These groups, unlike state or local chapters, are usually not separate associations, but rather groups within an association that have jurisdiction over an area of interest, rather than a geographic area.[14] These sections usually have a governing body, and the sections dues are either included in the members' regular dues or a separate fee is required.[15]

Councils and sections enable members who share a common occupational interest or professional specialty to exchange ideas and techniques unique to their area. In addition, many sections and councils provide members with educational opportunities, publications, and representation for the profession. Often sections and councils also provide the parent association with a training ground for future association leaders.

The American Physical Therapy Association (APTA) has 19 nationwide special-interest sections that provide a forum for physical therapists and physical therapist assistants. The APTA's sections include, for example, acute care/hospital clinical practice, administration, aquatic physical therapy, cardiopulmonary, geriatrics, and sports physical therapy. On the other hand, the American Trucking Associations (ATA) offer members seven councils ranging from the safety management council to the sales and marketing council.

The councils and sections of associations provide an additional vehicle to target specialties within professions and sectors within an industry.

INTERNATIONAL ASSOCIATIONS

A growing trend is international associations. These associations include those headquartered in the United States with foreign affiliates as well as associations located in foreign countries. It is estimated that 11 percent of associations have chapters in other countries, while 33 percent of associations maintain international affiliates.[16] The *Encyclopedia of Associations/International Organizations*, published by Gale Research, lists over 11,000 nonprofit organizations that are international in scope, membership, or interest, including multinational and binational groups and national associations headquartered outside of the United States. Examples of such international associations include the World Federation for Medical Information, based in Scotland, which promotes the integrated study of medical education worldwide and evaluates the effectiveness of medical education in meeting the needs of contemporary society, and the World Modeling Association, based in San Angelo, Texas, which fosters integrity and high standards of performance in the modeling and fashion merchandising industries in 10 countries.

According to the U.S. Department of Commerce, one-third of manufacturing companies now export. As American companies continue to explore global opportunities, international associations provide marketing access through trade shows and pavilions. For companies seeking international exposure, associations can provide a vital link that can save both money and time by sharing the lessons of those that have gone before.

All signs point to a continuing trend toward associations with an international flavor; it is estimated that 9 percent of national associations now translate their membership materials into other languages, including Spanish (77 percent), French (38 percent), German (16 percent) and Japanese (15 percent).[17]

ASSOCIATION SPECIALIZATION

A growing trend in associations and professional societies is membership specialization, where large associations form smaller affiliates that represent specialists within a larger industry, or new associations are formed to represent new or growing specialties. There are 400 national associations that represent banking and finance, 700 that represent business, 500, education, 800, manufacturing, and 1,100, national science associations listed in the directory, *National Trade and Professional Associations of the U.S.* Although some associations represent overlapping memberships, most of the associations represent specialized groups within larger industries.

While the marketing profession, for example, is represented by the 49,000-member American Marketing Association, an additional 125 associations represent sectors of the marketing profession at the national level alone:*

Armed Forces Marketing Council	Association of Incentive Marketing
Bank Marketing Association	Direct Marketing Association
Direct Marketing Association	Marketing Research Association

---

*Source: *National Trade and Professional Associations of the U.S.* Columbia Books, © 1993. Used with permission.

Medical Marketing   Mass Marketing Insurance
Association   Institute

Nonprofit Marketing Network   National Law Firm Marketing
                                     Association

Telemarketing Managers   Sales & Marketing Executives
Association   International

And, while the 300,000-member American Medical Association is the principal spokesman for the U.S. medical profession,
with over 2,000 local and regional medical societies, an estimated
750 specialized medical associations exist at the national level
alone, including:*

Aerospace Medical   Aging Association
Association
                                     American Burn Association
Ambulance Association
                                     American Fracture Association
American Epilepsy Society
                                     American Pain Society
American Heart Association
                                     Anxiety Disorders Association
American Thyroid Society
                                     Movement Disorder Society
Eye Bank Association of
America   Shock Society

National Rural Health
Association

When exploring the association market, it is critical to recognize the wide diversity of associations that may represent an industry. For almost any target market, whether businesses or
individuals, there likely exists an association that represents its
desired prospects. The more specific your prospecting becomes,
the greater your chances of success.

ASSOCIATION BUDGETS

While many associations have budgets that rival their corporate
partners, most associations are in fact small businesses; 80 percent of associations have fewer than 20 employees and annual
budgets of less than $1 million (see Exhibit 2–2).

---

*Source: *National Trade and Professional Associations of U.S.* Columbia Books, © 1993.
Used with permission.

EXHIBIT 2–2

Associations by Budget Size

Size of Budget	Percent United States Associations
$1–5 million +	22.0
$250,000–$1 million	20.6
$25,000–$250,000	29.1
0–$25,000	22.9
No information	5.4

Source: *National Trade and Professional Associations of the U.S.* Columbia Books, © 1993. Used with permission.

EXHIBIT 2–3

Ten Associations with Budgets in Excess of $25 Million

American Bankers Association
American Association for the Advancement of Science
American Bar Association
American Chemical Society
American Dental Association
American Trucking Associations
American Heart Association
American Institute of Architects
National Association of Realtors
National Education Association

Source: *Encyclopedia of Associations*, 27th. ed. vol. 1–3, Part 1–3, ed. by Deborah M. Burek. Gale Research, Inc., © 1993. Reproduced by permission of publisher.

While smaller associations dominate the landscape, the growth of associations with budgets in excess of $5 million is accelerating. In 1980 only 100 national associations or societies had budgets in excess of $5 million; by 1990 this total had grown to more than 300 associations. In addition, many other associations now boast budgets in excess of $25 million (see Exhibit 2–3).

ASSOCIATION LOCATION

Associations are established to serve their memberships and are generally located where their members are located or where the members can be best represented. Many assume that most national associations are located in Washington, D.C., but, in fact, the nation's capital is home to only a third of national associations. Associations now represent the third largest employer in the Washington area, trailing only the federal government and tourism and employing over 85,000 workers. The Chicago and New York regions are home to 17 percent and 15 percent respectively of national associations, followed by Los Angeles, Philadelphia, Boston, Dallas, San Francisco, and Detroit.[18] (See Exhibit 2–4.)

Like their for-profit counterparts, many national associations are lowering their operating costs by relocating to suburban areas from their traditional city locales. Today secondary cities are home to a growing number of national associations:*

Arlington, Texas–American Association of Public Health Physicians; Bowling Proprietors Association of America; Broker Management Council; Computer Aided Manufacturing-International; Computer Use in Social Services Network; Manufacturers Representatives of America; National Independent Automobile Dealers Association.

University Park, Pennsylvania–American Association of Professors of Yiddish; American Posological Society; Association of African Studies Programs; Association of Health Occupation Teacher Educators; Society of Experimental Psychologists; University Council for Educational Administration.

State and regional associations are generally located in the area where their members are located and tend to be concentrated near urban centers, airport hubs, and state capitals to facilitate transportation and representation.

---

*Source: *National Trade and Professional Associations of the U.S.* Columbia Books, © 1993. Used with permission.

EXHIBIT 2–4
National Association Headquarters

	Metropolitan Area			
Year	*New York*	*Washington*	*Chicago*	*Elsewhere*
1971	26%	19%	15%	40%
1972	25	20	15	40
1973	26	24	16	34
1974	25	24	17	34
1975	24	26	16	34
1976	23	27	16	36
1977	22	26	16	36
1978	22	27	16	35
1979	23	28	13	36
1980	21	28	14	37
1981	20	29	15	36
1982	19	30	15	36
1983	19	30	14	37
1984	19	31	18	32
1985	18	30	18	34
1986	17	31	18	34
1987	16	31	18	35
1988	16	32	18	34
1989	15	32	17	36
1990	15	32	17	36
1991	15	31	17	37
1992	15	31	17	37

Of the 7,500 U.S. organizations listed in this directory, over 30 percent are now located in the Washington area, 15 percent in the New York area, and 17 percent in and around Chicago. The rest are scattered, with Atlanta, Cleveland, Denver, Indianapolis, Los Angeles, Philadelphia, and San Francisco having small concentrations.

Source: *National Trade and Professional Associations of the U.S.* Columbia Books, © 1993. Used with permission.

ASSOCIATION SUBSIDIARIES

Approximately 17 percent of associations have formed for-profit subsidiaries, commonly called *service corporations*.[19] These subsidiaries are often established to conduct business that requires more active association marketing and to support activities outside of conventional association roles. Subsidiaries provide the association a vehicle to offer members creative and innovative programs, separate the liabilities and assets of the association, and add necessary program and management expertise.[20]

Associations are careful to ensure that the corporations remain "in the family"; in fact, 87 percent of the subsidiaries are wholly owned by the association parent, and members of the association's board also serve on the subsidiary's board of directors 89 percent of the time.[21] The most common income-producing activities of association subsidiaries are insurance programs (43 percent), publishing (21 percent), data processing (19 percent), industry promotion/advertising and mailing-list sales (15 percent), financial services and consulting (13 percent), and product sales (11 percent).[22]

ASSOCIATION FOUNDATIONS

In addition to subsidiaries and affiliates, the ASAE estimates that 35 percent of associations have established separate foundations.[23] Association-sponsored foundations are separate nonprofit organizations that support the purposes and goals of their association and provide the association with an additional source of nondues income for activities, including educational programs, research, training, and scholarships.[24]

Foundations provide an association another method to expand member services by attracting income, via tax-deductible donations, from outside of the association, including grants, corporate contributions, and nonmember donations.

ASSOCIATION MULTIMANAGEMENT

While most associations are managed by full- or part-time association staff, smaller associations often lack the resources to provide ongoing member support and therefore rely on association management companies to provide membership services.

Through the sharing of resources, association management companies provide services to several or many associations, including public relations, member communications, meeting and convention planning, government relations, and member education. According to the Institute of Association Management Companies, multimanagement permits associations to pay only for services needed, rather than be burdened with full-time expertise for part-time requirements.

It has been estimated that 400 association management companies now manage 3,000 associations. These companies represent an additional conduit to reach associations and their members.

THE BOTTOM LINE

As you examine the association market, your success will depend largely on how targeted your marketing becomes. Understanding the structure of an association is only the first step toward understanding how it makes decisions and who it influences.

NOTES

1. Howard Oleck, *Nonprofit Corporations, Organizations, and Associations*, 5th ed. (Prentice Hall, 1988), p. 938.
2. Michael O'Neil, *The Third America* (Jossey Bass, 1989), p. 161.
3. Barry Schimel, *100 Ways to Prosper in Today's Economy* (Acropolis Books, 1991), p. 211.
4. American Society of Association Executives, *The National-Chapter Partnership* (ASAE, 1993), p. 9.
5. *The National-Chapter Partnership*, p. 9.
6. American Society of Association Executives, *Policies and Procedures in Association Management* (ASAE, 1992) p. 9.
7. American Society of Association Executives, *Fundamentals of Association Management* (ASAE, 1982), p. 23.
8. *Policies and Procedures in Association Management*, p. 9.

9. *Fundamentals of Association Management*, p. 25.
10. *Policies and Procedures in Association Management*, p. 9.
11. *Fundamentals of Association Management*, p. 24.
12. *Policies and Procedures in Association Management*, p. 7.
13. Ibid. p. 77.
14. *The National-Chapter Partnership*, p. 11.
15. *Policies and Procedures in Association Management*, p. 78.
16. Ibid. p. 10.
17. Ibid. p. 76.
18. *Trade and Professional Association of the U.S.*, 28th ed. (Columbia Books, 1993), p. 16.
19. *Policies and Procedures in Association Management*, p. 4.
20. Jerald Jacobs *Association Law Handbook* (Bureau of National Affairs, 1986) pp. 430–431.
21. Mary McLean and Tracy Hulin, *Subsidiary Mini-Survey* (ASAE, 1991), p. 2.
22. Ibid. p. 22.
23. *Policies and Procedures in Association Management*, p. 5.
24. Isla Whittemore, "Associations Build Foundations," *Association Management*, (November 1981), p. 79.

Chapter Three

Inside the Association

Looking at the future, I think there is no question that the role of trade and professional associations will be enhanced. They will be more closely under the scrutiny of their members, they will be expected to deliver more, and their members will be more involved.[1]

Associations represent a different culture from the corporate sales or marketing culture. Your success in the association market will depend largely on how you are able to walk in the shoes of the association; for the more you understand their concerns and motivations, the greater your success in selling the association and its members.

THE ORGANIZATION

An association is composed of two vital components, its staff and its membership. The association is headed by an individual who is hired by the association's volunteer leadership and usually carries the title of president, executive vice president, or executive director. The chief of staff is usually selected based on a combination of factors, including knowledge of the association's businesses or profession, experience in managing associations, and knowledge of those who regulate or influence the business of the members. In associations that represent highly regulated industries or professions, the chief staff executive is often a former government or regulatory employee, while less-regulated associations may be represented by a leader chosen from the membership.

The chief of staff is usually responsible for promoting and furthering the objectives of the association and extending its membership and influence. The roles of the chief of staff often include the hiring and directing of staff, budget responsibility, representing the association to other associations and public and government agencies, and, perhaps most importantly, "ensuring that the needs of all members are met within the limits of the association's finances and the directives of the board."[2]

An association's staff usually includes second tier professionals often called program managers, directors, or vice presidents and supporting staff such as secretaries and administrative assistants. The number and nature of second tier staff depends on the activities of the association. In larger associations there is usually an individual in charge of each primary area, such as communications, member services, membership, education, government relations, convention, and public relations, while in smaller associations it is common to find people wearing many hats and the job titles confusing at best. In fact, according to the Association Operating Ratio Report compiled by the ASAE, the average association employs 20 full-time employees.[3]

Association members elect the volunteer leadership to oversee the association. An association is usually headed by a volunteer, often elected annually, called president, or, if the chief of staff has the title of president, chairman. The president presides at major meetings of the association, appoints members of the association's committees, and testifies on behalf of the association. The membership also elects representatives to serve on the association's governing body, usually called a board of directors. The board is normally composed of 10–19 members, who serve an average two-year term.[4] The board of directors is usually responsible for budget approval, establishing association policies, hiring and evaluating the chief of staff, reviewing and evaluating the recommendations of committees, and establishing membership criteria.[5]

Nonprofit boards of directors differ from those of their for-profit counterparts in several ways. While corporate boards of directors are usually composed of both insiders (staff) and outsiders, nonprofit boards are usually composed entirely of outsiders, that is, nonemployees of the organization. In addition, most nonprofit boards of directors are larger than their corporate counterparts, due in part to the volunteer nature of the nonprofit and its need to involve as many members as possible. However, "in sum, the nonprofit board has a protective, supervisory role similar to that of the for-profit board. The nonprofit board protects donors and clients broadly construed, while its for-profit counterpart protects its stockholders."[6]

While the board of directors has ultimate fiduciary responsibility to govern the association, due to its size it generally meets only twice a year. Most associations, therefore, have a smaller executive committee that oversees the association in the board's absence. Typically the executive committee is composed of five members, including the volunteer president, president-elect, vice president, past president, secretary/treasurer, and the association's chief of staff (usually as ex-officio member).[7] The executive committee, due to its smaller size, can meet more frequently than the board and therefore makes most operational and services decisions.

The broader membership of an association participates through service on association committees and in the association's activities, such as seminars and conventions. Committees guide the association's primary activities and provide critical member input. The number of committees varies widely from association to association and depends largely on the primary functions of the association and to the extent to which it is member-driven. Many associations prefer to have dozens of committees to enable as many members as possible to participate, while others prefer fewer, larger committees. A recent survey found that associations have an average of 11 committees, the most common being budget/financial, membership, education, government affairs, publications, long-term planning, public relations, and convention.[8]

The two tier organizational structure of an association is both its greatest strength and greatest weakness in the development of new products and services. While the structure ensures that services are evaluated and member input is received, the same consensus decision-making structure prolongs the final decision, frustrating and occasionally infuriating the unsuspecting corporate suitor.

ASSOCIATION MOTIVATION

The job of an association executive is often viewed as an ideal one, for many assume that associations, as nonprofits, face no financial pressure and therefore executives can focus exclusively on social and political activities. Unfortunately, associations are not immune to the same bottom line pressures that any business or professional faces. If an industry is in recession, or members are merging or consolidating, their association will mirror the recession, merger, or consolidation pressures of the industry that it represents.

The "Ups and Downs" of Membership Dues

According to an ASAE study, the average association relies on dues to generate approximately 43 percent of its total revenue. Generally, the smaller the association, the greater the reliance on dues to fund its operations. While dues vary significantly, a recent survey found that professional associations charge their individual members either a flat annual fee averaging $165, or fees based on the size of the professional's business of $108–$340. Trade associations, on the other hand, charge their business members either a flat annual fee averaging $588, or a fee based on the size of the business of $820 to $22,500.[9]

The challenge is that when industries or professions confront tough times, often the first expense to go is association dues, often at the very same time that members are relying more heavily on the association's services. The association is left to fund the needs of many with the dues of only a few. In addition, in businesses facing consolidation, the larger "merged" member will usually pay less dues than the two separate members had paid, although the new entity's needs for the association's services often continue unabated.

The average association faces an annual membership turnover of 11 percent, and many local and professional associations face turnover rates that exceed 20 percent per year.[10] Therefore the first and most important management task of the association is to attract and retain members. While most associations will successfully attract and replace lost members, other associations

EXHIBIT 3–1
Association Recession Strategies Most Frequently Used

---

1. More aggressive management oversight of expenses.
2. Start new programs for income.
3. Aggressive marketing of products and services.
4. Eliminate unprofitable programs.
5. Increase dues.

Source: Schlegel & Associates. Survey conducted for *Association Trends*, © 1992. Used with permission.

represent consolidating industries and shrinking memberships, and their survival depends on their ability to adapt. For some associations the answer lies in merger with similar associations, while others, like their industry counterparts, will downsize, disappear, or adopt aggressive strategies both to retain members and to replace lost dues revenue. When association executives were asked, "How has your organization been dealing with the recession?" they revealed that associations generally favor the development and marketing of nondues programs to increasing member dues (see Exhibit 3–1).

While the economy's impact on professionals and businesses significantly affects membership attraction and retention, an association's policies and positions can also affect membership. When the policy-making body of the 400,000-member American Bar Association (ABA) took controversial legislative and policy positions at its 1992 Annual Meeting, 2,766 members resigned from the association. The ABA adopted three strategies to increase membership value: enhance the delivery of ABA services to members, explore opportunities to increase nondues revenue, and expand services to its state and local bar associations.[11]

The Growth of Nondues Revenue

Many associations, rather than ride the membership wave, have sought to diversify their revenues. Although dues continue to be the single largest component of association income, associations

EXHIBIT 3–2
Strategic Issues for the 90s

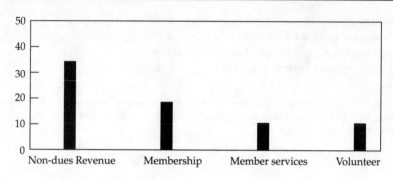

Source: *Lawrence-Leiter Report,* Lawrence-Leiter and Company, Kansas City, MO,
© 1990. Used with permission.

are decreasing their dependence on dues revenue and expanding their nondues income sources. In fact, over the past 10 years, dues income as a percentage of total income has declined by approximately one percent per year.[12] When 3,000 executives were informally polled about what they considered the two or three most important strategic issues facing associations in the 1990's, nondues revenue surpassed other concerns by two to one (see Exhibit 3–2).

The sources of association nondues income are as varied as the membership they represent, but the most significant contributors include convention registrations, advertising, publication sales, educational programs, expositions, and investment income. Other sources of nondues income on the rise include income earned by management or sponsorship of group insurance programs and royalties for the endorsement of products and services.

Associations pursue the development of programs and services and the nondues income they produce to satisfy other concerns:

Retain members. Membership retention is often based on whether members feel that the association is a good value for the dues paid. In tough economic times, members, whether businesses or individuals, examine all expenses and often evaluate the association's value by the "what have you done for me lately" test. Quality member services and programs have proven to increase membership renewal rates.

Michael T. Kulczycki, director of member services for the 2,500 member companies of the Automotive Service Industry Association (ASIA), says that "today members are seeking hardcore bottom line benefits to justify their dues; the social benefits are simply not enough." In response ASIA offers companies that manufacture, distribute, and sell motor vehicle parts and supplies a broad array of meetings, seminars, products, and services.

Attract members. Although membership in some associations is virtually required due to professional educational requirements or licensing, most associations represent only a fraction of their potential membership. Unfortunately, while an industry may gain through an association's efforts, the association is forced to survive on the dues of the fraction who join. Therefore associations often develop services to attract nonmembers to the association.

Services are another means of attracting members. While an association's legislative efforts on behalf of the industry or profession are often critical to a member's future, they are usually intangible. Services, on the other hand, are tangible and are viewed as more directly related to the member's pocketbook. When new members are asked why they have joined a particular association, they most frequently state that the association helps their business or practice. The association is constantly faced with the challenge of proving its worth to attract nonmembers and demonstrating its performance to retain members.[13]

The 54,000-member American Physical Therapy Association (APTA) has found that services that offer economic benefits "attract members looking for tangible products that impact their pocketbooks. Legislative issues are critical but they are often harder for 'checkbook' members to relate to," according to Sharon Meehan, APTA's director of component relations. The APTA offers its professional members a menu of information, career advancement opportunities, insurance programs, and financial services.

Image. Many associations have found that they have a "one issue" image. As that issue becomes less important to the membership, membership in the association is viewed as less critical and therefore dispensable. Member services can shine a tarnished image and make the association more attractive to both established and potential members.

Association differentiation. Most individuals and businesses belong to more than one association. Typically an individual will belong to a national society and local chapter, while businesses may belong to several umbrella organizations as well as state chapters and local chambers. The growing trend of association specialization is spawning new associations every day; associations that, in the past, represented an entire industry or profession are facing new association upstarts that represent industry sectors or occupational specialties. Therefore many associations develop member products or services to differentiate themselves from other, often competing, associations.

The Produce Marketing Association (PMA) represents companies that market fresh produce, including growers, shippers, distributors, processors, and supermarkets. The PMA recognizes that each of its members has multiple association options, since each represents a different segment within the produce marketing industry.

According to Ellen Peplinski, the PMA's manager of marketing, one of the keys of the PMA's success in member attraction and retention, "is our foundation, formed to promote increased consumption of produce through a program, co-sponsored with the National Cancer Institute, entitled "5 a day for better health"; the effort benefits all members and distinguishes us from the crowd." In addition, the PMA's convention and exposition attracts nearly 10,000 registrants from 30 countries. As an indication of its success, 47 percent of the PMA's funding is derived from its convention and exposition, 28 percent from training, education, and products, and only 25 percent from membership dues.

For-profit competition. Many associations are also facing increased competition in the delivery of core association services, such as education, conventions, and publications, from for-profit providers with greater marketing resources. Since these providers have no membership requirements, they can threaten an association that hasn't added other services. According to the Trade Show Bureau, for example, 95 percent of trade shows were produced by associations in 1975, versus only 55 percent in 1990, as for-profit providers gained market share from associations.

Reduce dues increases. One of the obvious responses to a shrinking membership is to increase dues on the remaining members. Unfortunately, at some point members may refuse to pay and revenue problems will accelerate. Through the development of products and services that generate nondues income, associations can often reduce the need for dues increases and are able to retain members.

Build a financial cushion. Unlike businesses, associations cannot easily raise capital in traditional investment markets. Nondues income enables associations to build a financial cushion for hard times and provide needed capital to permit expansion.

Kenneth Guenther, executive vice president of the 6,000-member Independent Bankers Association of America (IBAA), which represents community banks nationwide, states, "Services provide a revenue supplement for a trade association; it is growing harder to sustain an association on dues alone. The bottom line: services provide an association dual buffers of diversity, another source of operating income to compliment dues, and a better-rounded image to attract a broader array of members."

Continued ability to offer services. Nondues income enables associations to ensure continued provision of services in the face of membership volatility. For associations that rely on tax-deductible contributions from benefactors and face uncertain fundraising efforts, services provide an alternative base of income to ensure that critical needs are meet.

Associations and the IRS

While service development and the generation of nondues income are growing association desires, both the associations and the vendors courting them must understand the impact of IRS regulations on association activities. Because associations are nonprofit, tax-exempt organizations, their activities are restricted. While the IRS code identifies 23 types of tax-exempt organizations, associations and professional societies generally fall into two tax-exempt categories: 501 (c)(6) and 501 (c)(3).

Professional societies and associations of individuals are generally 501(c)(3) organizations. This status is generally more restrictive than 501(c)(6) organizations. C3 organizations often qualify for special nonprofit postage rates; since their activities are primarily educational, donations to C3 organizations are tax-deductible by the donor, and C3 organizations are often exempt from some state and local taxes.

Trade associations are generally formed as 501(c)(6) organizations. While C6 organizations generally do not have some of the restrictions on their activities as C3 organizations, they also don't share the same privileges either. A C6 organization, for example, does not usually enjoy preferred postal rates. On the other hand, trade associations are permitted to engage in both legislative and political activities related to the business interests of the members and are free to engage in other activities so long as the primary activity remains related to its mission.

While associations are tax exempt organizations, they are subject to tax on income that is unrelated to their mission or business (the unrelated business income tax); which may include some non-dues income. Associations may risk the loss of their tax exempt status if the income from unrelated businesses is excessive.

Royalties–The Best of Both

Royalties are income received by the association for use of a valuable association property right, usually its name and logo (akin to licensing in the corporate world). Royalty income is tax free (exempt from unrelated business income tax) and normally does not threaten an association's tax-exempt status. In order for the income to qualify as royalty income, associations cannot provide services, such as taking orders, designing direct mail, paying for postage, or providing advertising, in exchange for the income.

Although the association usually cannot actively market or sell a program or service and have the income treated as tax-exempt, it can support corporate marketing and use its communication channels (magazines, newsletters, memos, mailing lists, etc.) to promote the programs. In short, what associations do, and do well, is lend their credibility and goodwill to selected product or services. The association's authorization provides the opportunity to market programs with the association's "seal of approval."

It is important to note that while many associations prefer royalty income, others, either through the association or through a service corporation, may wish to take a more active marketing role.

THE FUTURE

For those willing to understand the association market, its motivations, and its membership's needs, association partnership opportunities abound.

NOTES

1. William F. Ouchi, *The M-Form Society* (Addison-Wesley, 1984), p. 32.
2. James Dunlop, *Leading the Association* (ASAE, 1989), pp. 101–102.
3. *Policy and Procedures in Association Management* p. 137.
4. Ibid. p. 17.
5. Dunlop, p. 104.
6. Sharon Oster, "Nonprofit Management: Is Managing 'Save the Children' Any Different from Managing General Motors?", *Yale Management* (Fall 1992), pp. 19–20.
7. *Policies and Procedures in Association Management*, p. 20.

  8. Ibid. p. 21.
  9. Ibid. pp. 83–87.
 10. Ibid. p. 73.
 11. James Podgers, "Which Way ABA?" *ABA Journal* (December 1992), pp. 62–63.
 12. *Association Operating Ratio Report* (ASAE, 1989), p. 3.
 13. The Foundation of the American Society of Association Executives, *The Decision to Join* (ASAE Foundation, 1981), p. 8.

Chapter Four

Successful Program Development

As you begin to evaluate the opportunities of association marketing, a look at the criteria and evaluation utilized by associations will enable you to identify those ideas worth pursuing and to develop proposals that meet the association's "litmus tests."

Any program will ultimately be evaluated by three parties: the member, the association, and the corporate partner. If a program is to succeed it will have to satisfy all three; if the company providing the program is not satisfied, it is likely that the members will receive poor service, the sales force will be unmotivated, and continued support of the program will be at risk. If the association is dissatisfied, its support of the program will wane, its advocacy will waiver, and its endorsement will be in jeopardy.

But above all, if the association's members are dissatisfied, both the association and its corporate partner will suffer. For if members feel that the program has failed, the association will be blamed for poor judgment and the members' dues often held "hostage," while members seek recourse from the provider. The association will quickly become the members' advocate and will subsequently view the program as "not worth the time," or else risk the association's goodwill and loss of membership.

All parties of an association program seek benefits from the relationship. To succeed such programs should be viewed as "win-win," for a well designed program will be developed to benefit the association member and in turn will benefit the association and the provider. If the primary beneficiary is viewed as the association or the provider, the seeds of failure have been planted.

WIN-WIN PROGRAMS

The Association Member

Lower costs—Most association programs offer members lower costs than they could obtain on individual bases. If the program is easily available elsewhere at the same price, then the member will often conclude that the association has negotiated poorly or, worse, that since the members gained nothing, the association must be "making a killing."

Improved, more targeted product—The redesign or packaging of a product to meet the unique needs of the association's members. The inclusion of items which are often options, such as extended warranties, unique payment terms, or the exclusion of irrelevant features can often be viewed as being as important as price concessions.

Improved access—Association programs often provide members improved access to products or services that would be difficult to obtain on an individual basis. Access can be the basis of excellent program development, for if a product is difficult to obtain or is viewed as available only to members able to purchase in large quantities, the association can improve access by serving the association as a single purchasing entity.

Increased confidence—An association program enables members to buy with the confidence that the association has selected, negotiated, and is offering a specific product on their behalf. A purchase through an association program should also provide members greater recourse if the product or service fails to perform as promised.

Pride—Members also want to view their usage of the association's programs as support for the association and for other members. This affinity is one of the key elements to the successful marketing of any association program.

The Association

Membership value—Programs are evaluated based on the extent to which they add value to membership. Programs that address the needs of members and are related to the association's mission meet the test. Increasing the value of association membership is critical in the association's drive to attract nonmembers and retain its existing members.

Association differentiation—If the association competes for members with other associations that may represent specialty member segments, programs offer the opportunity to amplify the benefits of membership. Product offerings also tend to improve the image of associations since they are often viewed as more innovative and forward-looking.

Visibility—Services can offer associations opportunities to increase their visibility and to attract members. Often the sales force of corporate partners "sell" the association, while selling the service that is endorsed. The association gains an advocate, while the partner gains a sale.

Nondues income—Most programs offer the association an opportunity to generate nondues income. The income is often an ongoing revenue based on the results of sales activity but may also be a lump-sum endorsement fee.

The Partner

Increased market share—By targeting both marketing and promotion activities, market penetration should increase with the added leverage of the association's "seal of approval."

Lower acquisition and retention costs—Depending on the product or service and the role the association plays in your marketing, your cost to acquire new business should be lower, since marketing is targeted and member affinity should reduce sales calls and expense.

Image—The association's endorsement can increase a company's image within an industry or profession. Such an image boost can increase market penetration and provide the key to enter a new market.

Cross-sell—Most companies offer more products than those offered through the association's program, and often the company finds that the association's goodwill rubs off on other services.

THE "INSIDE" CRITERIA

Associations should be viewed as custodians of the association's goodwill, and nothing can destroy that faster than programs that don't deliver and companies that don't perform as promised. Therefore associations don't take the endorsement of companies lightly.

Associations know the endorsement of a product or service will be seen by many as an endorsement of the supplier.[1] Therefore the association's evaluation will not only include a review of the proposed service but also of the capability of the supplier to fulfill the promises made. Before discussing the specific opportunities that are available, it is important to review the criteria used by associations to evaluate proposals. Knowledge of the "inside" criteria will help you determine partnership opportunities and select the ideal association.

1. Does the service or product advance the mission of the association and meet the needs of the membership? All associations are established to advance the businesses or interests of members they represent. A service which assists members to operate more profitably or efficiently will be viewed as advancing the association's mission, as opposed to products which simply provide the association with an added revenue stream. For, "the most successful nondues programs are motivated as much by member needs as return on investment."[2]

"Without question, our number one consideration is: is the program or service consistent with the image of the association and does it offer a service that the membership needs?" says Terence J. Furlong, senior vice president of marketing for the American Trucking Associations (ATA). The ATA, which represents 4,000 trucking firms, provides its members a catalog that displays the associations' products, publications, and services. Each time that members choose materials from the catalog, "they not only are buying the most up-to-date products available but are helping to support the services, knowledge, and expertise that the association provides to the industry," says Furlong.

2. Does the service leverage the strengths and expertise of the association? To the extent that a service is viewed as a natural

outgrowth of the association's prior efforts, that service will be viewed more favorably. Such service extensions by an association will be easier for the staff to support and for the membership to understand and accept.

Mark French, president of French & Associates, a Washington, D.C. marketing consultant to associations, points out that "it may seem obvious, but successful association programs are those that are viewed as an integral part of the association. For programs that are too far afield are not likely to be successful and often quickly become a distraction to the association. Successful programs are those that are viewed as meeting a need, not services that are looking for a need to fill."

3. Does the program offer unique features unavailable outside of the association? Generally an association will not consider a service or product that can be easily purchased elsewhere under the same conditions. Associations seek products or services that can be marketed as a member benefit and are available only through the association. The key is to design a program that recognizes the association's members' aggregate purchasing power and their specific needs.

4. Is there a tangible benefit to members? Such tangible benefits can include lower pricing that recognizes the group's aggregate purchasing power (not available to the members who would normally purchase without the benefit of such volume discounts) or improved access to programs that would not be readily available to individual members. Remember, associations are seeking ways to attract members; an ideal service or product is one that will serve as a magnet for nonmembers to join the association.

Associations are growing increasingly wary of programs that offer discounts from list prices on products that can be purchased "over-the-counter." With the popularity of office superstores and "clubs," associations are careful not to offer products that members may be able to purchase locally at lower prices and on similar terms.

5. What is the demand for the service or product and what are its chances of success? Services are viewed more favorably if they solve member problems or address member needs. To the extent that services address member "hotbuttons," the odds of success are increased.

An association's comfort is increased if the company proposing the service has a track record with other associations and with the association's members and provides a comprehensive marketing plan. Christopher W. Seidel, vice president of member services for the National Association of Realtors, says that "the services that an association sponsors must be viewed as significant to the membership. Successful services are those that are based on solid market research to assure they meet member needs."

6. What management and staff time is needed? Is the service or program turnkey to the extent that the company exhibits its ability to support its marketing and sales efforts? Is the company viewed by the association as a provider of solutions or as a bearer of problems? If a vendor enhances the association and provides answers to membership problems, the program will be preferred to proposals that require constant staff support and marketing assistance.

7. Does the program help the association attract and retain members? If the association's members have many association options from which to obtain the existing benefits of membership, the association will often seek services that can differentiate it from others and act as a catalyst for membership.

"Association services can act as golden handcuffs by providing a powerful incentive to attract members and a very effective method of retaining them," says Arlene Sirkin, president of Washington Resource Consulting Group, a Washington, D.C. area-based association marketing consultant.

8. What is the goodwill risk? Regardless of the potential revenue, associations will evaluate the risk to the association if the service fails. While the risk may be minimal in most services, risks can be considerable in the delivery of financial services and insurance programs, where a member's money may be at risk.

9. What is the potential revenue? Associations will generally evaluate a program based on its ability to generate income while achieving other association goals, such as membership attraction or retention. Like businesses, associations have limited resources and seek to support those services or programs that can produce reasonable revenues in relation to the efforts required and the risks incurred (resources and especially its goodwill).

10. The bottom line of evaluation: Is the association willing to brand the product or service with its name and "marry" the company? If all the evaluation goes well, this is the "yes" you are seeking.

Recognizing the criteria an association will utilize, we can examine the many association partnership opportunities that are available, including group purchasing, insurance programs, financial services, and educational and information programs.

SUCCESSFUL PROGRAM DEVELOPMENT "INSIDE" CHECKLIST

1. Does the service or program advance the mission of the association?

2. Does the service leverage the strengths or expertise of the association?

3. Does the program have unique features, unavailable outside the association?

4. Does the program offer tangible benefits to the membership?

5. What is the demand for the service and its chances of success?

6. What association management and staff time is needed?

7. How does the program help the association attract and retain members?

8. What is the goodwill risk to the association?

9. What is the potential revenue to the association?

10. Is the association willing to "marry" the company?

THE BOTTOM LINE

Associations seek programs that enable the association to attract and retain members by offering services that add membership value and generate nondues income.

NOTES

1. Mirlam Meister, "Marketing Sponsored Products and Services," *Marketing the Nonprofit Association* (GWSAE Foundation, 1992), p. 181.
2. Mark French, "Nondues Ventures," *Executive Update* (June 1992), p. 23.

Chapter Five

Group-Purchasing Opportunities

Most associations represent individual professionals or businesses, many of which are small businesses. These members share common traits, regardless of their industry or occupation: generally they are at a distinct disadvantage over their larger industry counterparts because they are unable to obtain quantity pricing on the products and services they need in order to effectively compete or operate.

However, when these same members are viewed as part of a larger association of buyers or prospects with similar needs, they represent a significant opportunity to reach a target market of prospects, which not only share common product and service needs but are often motivated by a common bond, exhibited by their involvement and dues paying in the association. The key is to recognize the members' needs and develop programs which provide leverage unavailable without the association. Such program development will ensure strong member acceptance and utilization.

GROUP PURCHASING-PROGRAM CRITERIA

The range of group purchasing opportunities is limited only by your recognition of the needs of each association membership. Almost any product or service that can be delivered individually can be packaged and delivered to an association membership. The key is to review the product and company characteristics which are often common to successful group-purchasing programs:

Can the product or service benefit through increased sales and can those benefits be passed on to the program purchasers? In the typical sales environment, price is often contingent on the quantity purchased and the quantity is usually determined in advance or at the time of sale. The challenge in the association market is that associations will not guarantee a minimum level of sales, so the company must evaluate the clout of the association and the potential sales volume. In addition, rather than sales being generated from one customer, the association's members usually order on an individual basis from, potentially, thousands of locations nationwide. Therefore, savings are more difficult to quantify.

Can the company identify the buyers of its products? While the answer may seem obvious, many companies, in fact, lack a unified system that permits the tracking of sales by the type of business, profession, decision maker, or by the product's application. The greater the corporation's ability to track sales and profile buyers, the greater its ability to target the association market and develop programs that meet member needs.

Don't overlook the value of your sales force, for while the corporation may lack a sophisticated tracking system, your sales staff certainly knows who its hot prospects are and what characteristics they have in common.

Do the product's current sales and marketing efforts fit the association membership delivery needs, and, if not, can they be modified? While the concept of group purchasing seems simple enough, companies must be able to ensure that the pricing and the products offered can be delivered. For example, if an association has members nationwide but the vendor is capable of supporting sales only in a certain region, members will be left with unfulfilled promises. In addition, if the vendor permits each region to establish its own pricing, a negotiated nationwide association price will create inequities and certain disappointments among the membership and the company sales force.

Can the product be delivered to provide member value beyond, or in addition to, price? Often vendors limit their vision of association programs to ones that simply deliver lower prices. For example, an association program could include product enhancements or a package customized to meet member needs. Additional benefits could enhance the program and differentiate it from programs available outside of the association; examples of such benefits include: leasing options for major purchases, extended warranty options, and unique credit or installment purchase arrangements.

While no specific association group-purchasing program is considered "typical," most programs share basic characteristics that can serve as the basis for program development and case history discussion. The players in an association group-purchasing program are, of course, the association, the member, and the company.

The association evaluates and then endorses the products or services of companies which meet its criteria and member needs. In exchange for its endorsement the association usually receives non-dues income, often referred to as royalties in recognition of the value of its name and logo in marketing the program to its members. The association often also gains an improved image among its members and a vehicle to attract and retain membership.

Based on the association's evaluation of the company and its products, the member gains buying confidence and receives lower pricing and/or improved access to the products or services. The member's view of the association is enhanced and the benefit of membership increased as he obtains benefits unavailable outside of the association. The odds of membership renewal are thus increased.

The corporate partner gains access to a target market of prospects who share buying habits and are motivated by a respect for the association that has earned their dues. The company also gains the opportunities to reduce marketing costs by focusing its efforts, to increase the quality of its prospects, to simplify the prospects' decision-making processes, and to increase market share.

The ideal program is a partnership that helps all parties achieve their respective goals.

Business Forms and Supplies

Most association members are small businesses or individual professionals who generally purchase business supplies over-the-counter at near-list prices. By aggregating the needs of an association's membership, individual members can gain increased access to a wider variety of supplies and are able to purchase individually at quantity prices. The member saves money and the supplier gains market share.

According to one survey conducted by the ASAE, 13 percent of associations now provide a business form or supplies group-purchasing program to their members. It is interesting to note that while approximately 20 percent of local, state, and regional associations now offer programs, only 4 percent of national associations offer such programs today.[1]

In the late 1980s, the retail office supply stores of Jacobs Gardner began to confront increased competition from office supply superstores. Rather than simply lower prices, in 1989 Jacobs Gardner established a new program, Penny Wise, to offer office supplies via direct response channels. In 1991, Penny Wise began to pursue relationships with associations to market their products to members nationwide. They offer association members access to over 18,000 office supply products at prices not available on an individual basis. While many members might have access to office supply superstores, the Penny Wise catalog offers an expanded array of products and free delivery (see Exhibit 5–1).

Jodie Hirsch, director of association sales and marketing at Penny Wise, says that "our initial response has been very strong, with over 160 associations enrolled in the first 18 months of the program." While the response of the associations has been encouraging, the bottom line to Penny Wise is account acquisition and ultimately sales. "Our acquisition costs have proven to be lower through joint marketing with associations, and our average sale is consistently higher. Plus, associations enable us to convert higher volume businesses than our typical retail buyer."

Penny Wise has found that its ideal association prospects are those that represent the small businesses or professional firms similar to their existing nonmember customer base. Penny Wise also seeks associations where the members have a strong affinity and groups interested in providing and supporting member services, not simply establishing an income stream. Jodie Hirsch states, "We strive to offer programs that provide real membership value and associations, based on actual sales, with sufficient

EXHIBIT 5–1
Penny Wise Office Products Member Advertisement

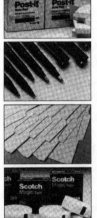

Members Now Have 18,000 Ways to Save on Office Products.

Penny Wise offers 18,000 brand name supplies at guaranteed lowest prices — from 20% to 81% off retail! Plus, we pass along extra savings to all members. This means Penny Wise is simply the easiest, most cost-effective way to save money on office products!

- **Save Up to an Additional 11% with Your Association Discount.**
- Guaranteed Lowest Price. • Easy to Order, Easy to Return.
- Free Delivery, Anywhere in the Continental U.S. (Minimum $25 Order).
- Same Day Credit Approval.

Call toll-free now for your FREE full color catalog. . .
ask for our FREE PC software for computer ordering.

1-800-942-3311
(301-699-1000 in the Washington, DC area)

PENNY·WISE OFFICE PRODUCTS

NOTE: For the ad above, please use the alphabet to create your acronym. Place it above 'Members', left justified, as the first line of the headline. In either ad, please insert your logo to the right of the Penny Wise logo.

A B C D E F G H I
J K L M N O P Q
R S T U V W X Y Z
A B C D E F G H I
J K L M N O P Q
R S T U V W X Y Z
A A A A A A N N
N N N S S S S S

Members Now Have 18,000 Ways to Save on Office Products

Penny Wise offers 18,000 brand name supplies at guaranteed lowest prices — from 20% to 81% off retail! Plus, we pass along extra savings to all members. This means Penny Wise is simply the easiest, most cost-effective way to save money on office products!

- **Save Up to an Additional 11% with Your Association Discount.**
- Guaranteed Lowest Price. • Easy to Order, Easy to Return.
- Free Delivery, Anywhere in the Continental U.S. (Minimum $25 Order).
- Same Day Credit Approval.

Call toll-free now for your FREE full color catalog. . .
ask for our FREE PC software for computer ordering.

1-800-942-3311
(301-699-1000 in the Washington, DC area)

PENNY·WISE OFFICE PRODUCTS

Used with the permission of Penny Wise Office Products.

compensation while maintaining a profit margin adequate to support our ongoing marketing efforts."

Every business needs one or more standard business forms to conduct its sales, marketing, accounting, or governmental reporting functions. While many associations today help members interpret new regulations, other associations also provide, in conjunction with vendors, standard forms that make the members' tasks easier and more affordable.

The 4,200-member National Association of College Stores represents the $6.4 billion college store industry. The association's members serve nearly 95 percent of America's 13 million college students. As its members have evolved from mere college bookstores to sophisticated retail operations, their membership needs have changed as well. The association now provides a broad range of publications, products, and services that are specific to the needs of college stores, including standardized and customized forms.

Business Equipment

While many association members now have access to general office equipment through office supply warehouses and superstores, they generally have fewer options on the purchase of more specialized business equipment. Associations that represent these specialized groups are often receptive to programs that recognize their members' potential purchasing volume. Such programs provide access to products and pricing unavailable on an individual basis and provide the member with tangible evidence of the value of association membership. Meanwhile, the association's members are able to short-cut the decision-making process with the added confidence provided by the association's endorsement.

Association business equipment partnerships seem certain to increase, as only 12 percent of associations now offer group-purchasing programs that include business equipment. While local, state, and regional associations are more likely to have such purchasing programs than their national counterparts, such programs are being offered equally by professional and business associations.[2]

Pitney Bowes, the leading manufacturer of postage meters and mailing equipment, is actively expanding its association marketing programs. Having begun with hospital associations, Pitney Bowes is now targeting a variety of associations that represent small businesses, both to solidify and expand in existing markets and to penetrate under-represented markets. According to Andy Daigle, vice president of national/major accounts, "Small employers do not have the time or the in-house expertise to study or evaluate equipment. Many businesses, therefore, rely on their associations for such review and approval—essentially providing their 'seal of approval'."

Pitney Bowes has found that association programs motivate its sales force by providing quality leads and higher closing ratios. The key to Pitney Bowes' early successes, says Mr. Daigle, "is to take an active and visible role at all levels of the association, including trade shows, advertising, magazine articles, and targeted association promotions. In short, once you have won the endorsement, don't waste it."

With 4,700 sales people operating out of 65 districts across the country, Xerox's decision to enter the association market was motivated from the bottom up. "While we have always prospected among associations themselves, our sales force suggested we drive the benefits to the next level—the association's members. The decision was not an easy one, for while association programs have enormous potential, there are no sales commitments and no guarantees that the association will bring incremental sales to the table," said Bart Schramm, marketing and operations manager of Xerox's U.S. customer operations.

In late 1991, Xerox launched its Focused Partnership Program, which enables national associations that meet Xerox's criteria to offer its full product line of business copiers, laser printers, and, where applicable, its engineering products, to association members at significant savings. Each program is customized for the association based on membership needs and the marketing vehicles available within the association. According to Schramm, "The key to our success has been our team effort. We support our programs with advertising targeted at the association's membership, active trade show support, an active public relations campaign, and a motivated sales force."

As a testimonial to Xerox's success, the Focused Partnership Program was recently voted the best new program within Xerox's marketing group.

Specialized Services

Each industry or profession has needs which are specific to its businesses or occupations. Often, an association in conjunction with corporations can gain members both improved access and lower pricing, while providing the vendor the opportunity to increase market share.

When trucking companies were faced with the need to check and monitor the driving records of its drivers on a nationwide basis, the American Trucking Associations responded. The association endorsed DAC Services' "driver screening" service. The ATA-endorsed service provides member companies' driving records from all 50 states, instant employment history information, workers' compensation and injury records, criminal records, and consumer credit reports.

Recognizing the enormous up-front capital required to fully equip a new dental practice or update an existing practice, the 140,000-member American Dental Association (ADA) endorsed a leasing firm that provides members an alternative to purchasing the necessary equipment. "By working with a leasing firm that understands the needs of a dental practice, we were able to satisfy a real member need," according to Karen Hoyt, the ADA's director of membership development and services.

Computer Hardware/Software

With the rapid growth of personal computers has come savage price competition. Associations represent an untapped distribution network that can deliver increased sales—so long as the systems offered meet member needs. Through associations businesses have the opportunity to package systems customized to a very specific market, which often reduces the pressure to compete only on price. Associations represent a viable and proven network for the marketing of software, for each association represents specific industries or occupations that have software needs well beyond simply packaged word processing or spread sheets. With the "seal of approval" of an association, software can be private-labeled for each targeted membership.

The Air Conditioning Contractors Association of America provides its 3,000 members with a broad menu of technical publications, books, research assistance, and other services. Today, in conjunction with a software firm, the association offers software derived from four of its manuals for the design of air conditioning systems. The software is marketed in conjunction with the association's publications and is promoted within the manuals on which the software is based.

The association is now able to meet the informational needs both of members who are comfortable only with its manuals and of the growing membership that is computer friendly.

Freight/Overnight Mail

Today, faster is better. Both businesses and professionals need the efficiency of overnight mail services. But the same members are often faced with paying top price due to their individual small volumes. Some companies now enable associations to provide overnight mail services which harness the collective volume of the membership; the company gains market share and the members receive lower pricing.

The affinity marketing firm, Meridian One, of Alexandria, Virginia, offers associations the ability to provide members with overnight air express shipping at significant savings. According to Mike Quinn of Meridian One, "Through our corporate partner, member businesses have access to discount levels normally reserved for high volume shippers. The program has received a solid reception from over 200 associations ranging from trade associations to professional societies. Today, associations are one of the fastest-growing market segments for air express carriers."

Meridian One targets associations that represent small to mid-size businesses or professionals who have regular shipping needs. To keep marketing costs in line, Meridian One offers two association programs, one designed for smaller associations that utilize generic marketing materials, the other for larger associations that provides customized promotional materials featuring the association's name or logo.

Based on its success, Meridian One now offers associations a menu of services in conjunction with various corporate partners, including long-distance service, prepaid legal services, and fax machines.

Long Distance and Communication Services

One of the fastest-growing areas of association programs is long-distance services. With the fierce competition of long-distance carriers, both direct providers and resellers, the search for alternative marketing channels has focused on associations. Through associations, long-distance carriers are able to offer lower pricing to members by considering the aggregate usage of the membership. Since much of business long-distance usage is daytime, association membership is a potential source of more profitable business. Also, since most are smaller businesses, association members will likely be solid, long-term customers who are less likely to take advantage of alternative options that bypass traditional carriers.

According to a 1991 survey of associations, 12 percent offered a telephone group-purchasing program to their members. As evidence of their popularity, telephone programs are being offered at approximately the same frequency by state, local, regional, and national associations and by both individual and business member associations.[3]

Sprint, the nation's third-largest long-distance provider, entered the association market in 1987 in order to increase sales and maintain its existing market share. Through its association program, Sprint targets trade associations that represent businesses with strong long-distance usage patterns. Debra Kaplan Gibbs, group manager of Sprint's Association Program, states that "association programs have proven their worth, since the association's affinity has both increased our market share and, more importantly, significantly reduced account turnover versus non-association business."

One of the keys to Sprint's success is a dedicated association telemarketing campaign. With the heated competition among long-distance carriers, "Direct mail may provide an introduction, but telemarketing is critical to the close," says Sprint's Debra Gibbs. Since some associations are hesitant to have their members called by someone outside of the association, Sprint invites associations to approve the scripts, conduct a test of the calls, and tour the telemarketing facility.

Sprint is quick to admit that successful association programs must be a team approach. The association must be committed to supporting the program's marketing and promotion, and the provider must have a dedicated sales and support system. One of Sprint's communication vehicles is the distribution of a newsletter for its associations. The newsletter discusses marketing successes, new associations, and new products and services. Gibbs sums it up, "If you don't work it, it won't work." See Exhibit 5–2.

While the members of associations are the targets of most of the marketing, associations themselves are heavy users of long distance and communication services to reach their members. Often programs designed to attract an association's members will also attract the business of the association. Associations that use the services they support not only endorse the program but become its advocates and give testimony to its quality and value.

The future of association communication services is likely to expand quickly as members utilize broadcast fax and e-mail services. In addition, in early 1993 customers will be able to change their long-distance carriers without changing their 800 numbers; the industry refers to this as "portability." Portability will accelerate long-distance competition as businesses who may have previously resisted switching, fearing the need to change their 800 phone numbers, will feel free to change their long-distance carriers.

Airlines

The U.S. Travel Data Center estimates that over 200 million business and convention trips were taken in 1990 alone. There is no doubt that associations are a major contributor to this traffic; for every meeting scheduled there are members who need airline reservations. Many airlines have recognized the influence of

EXHIBIT 5–2
Sprint's Association Newsletter (Member Benefit News)

Member Benefit NEWS

Sprint

Volume I, No. 2   A Quarterly Publication for Sprint Member Benefit Program Partners   Summer 1992

The Sprint Member Benefit Program is Better than Ever!

The special 5% member discount can now be applied to Sprint's newest business product, Sprint CLARITY℠. This service is the product of choice for:

1. Businesses that spend between $1,000 and $40,000 per month in long distance and want maximum volume discounts.

2. Multi-location organizations that need billing flexibility and would like all their locations' usage combined for greater savings.

3. Companies with both outbound and inbound (800) service, that want just one invoice and combined volume discounts.

CLARITY offers a simplified rate structure and 6 second billing for all calling, including FONCARD and international usage.

What's Inside

2 ....Inside Sales Rep of the Month

2 ....New FONCARD With Easy Features

3 ....Sprint/Centel Proposed Merger

3 ....Int'l Travelers Use Sprint Express

3 ....Sprint Sets Quality Standard

4 ....Sprint Sets Quality Standard (cont.)

4 ....Sprint Facts

As part of the CLARITY program, organizations will also receive additional discounts on Sprint's Broadcast FAX and Document on Demand products and Conference Calling service.

Your members can learn more about CLARITY, by calling 1 (800) 473–0898 (7 am–7 pm CST) and requesting a visit from their local Sprint Representative. ◆

Which Long Distance Company Does Your Headquarters Use?

Your members belong to your association for many different reasons. One of the main ones is for information and guidance that pertains to their business or interests. When members have questions, they trust your judgement and recommendations.

When you recommend Sprint to your members, you are sending them a message. Yet, when your members call and ask what long distance company your headquarters uses and it isn't Sprint, you send a conflicting message.

As an endorser of the Sprint Member Benefit Program, why don't you consider switching your headquarter's long distance to Sprint? By switching after your program is in place, your

headquarters will be considered "new business" and will contribute to your royalties generated from the program. You also get to take advantage of the extra 5% savings! Most importantly, you'll send a consistent message to your members that not only do you endorse Sprint, but you also use Sprint, furthering your members' confidence in the program.

Besides just long distance, Sprint can help your headquarters run its business more efficiently. Sprint offers a spectrum of products ranging from Broadcast Fax Services to Video Conferencing. Sprint can help you communicate more effectively with your members.

Sprint is here not only to help you offer a valuable member benefit, but also to help with telecommunication solutions for your headquarters.

Switching is easy. Just contact your Member Benefit Program Account Manager, who will be happy to arrange an on-site visit by a Sprint Sales Rep. He or she will analyze your business and get you set up on the best product available for your headquarters. Don't worry about your 800 service. Keep it on your current carrier until March 1993, when you'll "own the number" and can designate what long distance company you want to carry the service. If you don't have an 800 number yet, you may want to consider looking into Sprint's low cost product, FONLINE 800℠. ◆

---

associations by seeking to become the "official airline" of the association or a specific association event.

The airline partnership typically provides members with price incentives and the association with free tickets, based on membership usage, fee freight, and VIP benefits such as travel upgrades. According to the ASAE's survey of Association Meeting Trends, 45 percent of associations that held annual conventions named an official air carrier that booked an average of 242 tickets.

United Airlines, the second-largest U.S.-based carrier, views association programs as an effective vehicle for attracting meeting business. According to Steve Praven, United's manager of meeting sales, "Through designation as an association's official carrier we can gain increased market share, the members may gain travel discounts, and the association benefits through complimentary tickets based on usage and discounts on freight, both of which reduce the association's revenue needs."

In addition to domestic travel needs of associations, as associations establish international affiliates and alliances, their members' international travel increases rapidly, attracting renewed interest among carriers. In addition, airlines are now expanding their relationships with associations, beyond meeting travel needs, to other products and services such as airline club memberships.

Travel Services

Associations are the leading provider of seminars, conferences, and conventions in America today. In 1991 alone, associations held 215,000 meetings that attracted nearly 23 million attendees.[4] Each of these events requires members to travel, and therefore associations can represent a significant conduit for marketing travel services. While many travel agencies have targeted the travel needs of the association, they usually overlook the travel of the association's members—the real market.

When Camelot Travel Services of Englewood, Colorado was launched in 1989, it recognized that associations have multifaceted needs that could only be served through a integrated approach. According to Camelot's Executive Vice President Daniel W. Bicker, most associations "have three travel needs: business travel of the association staff, member and staff travel to association meetings, and the individual travel needs of the members themselves. While other travel agencies have targeted the needs of association staff, they usually ignore the iceberg of potential that lies beneath the surface—the association's members."

Due in large part to its focused association strategy, Camelot Travel Services has grown to one of the top 150 travel agencies in the country in a field of 36,000 agencies. To continue its growth, Camelot targets associations that are national in scope and generate a minimum of $200,000 in travel annually. Recognizing that each association's organization and needs are unique, Camelot offers associations various program options, ranging from the endorsement of the agency to satellite remote ticketing printers at locales of higher volume associations.

Camelot Travel currently serves 70 associations but believes that the potential has just been scratched. "As the pressure grows on airline carriers to build traffic and profitability, travel costs will increase and association budgets will be directly affected. By combining the travel volume of the association and its members, the association gains the ability to negotiate better airline and hotel prices. The more segments of travel that the association can address, the greater its clout and the lower its prices," according to Camelot's Daniel Bicker.

Two trends bode well for association travel services: airlines are increasingly fighting for passenger loyalty internationally and domestically, and associations are increasingly becoming international in scope. Certainly, as associations gain international members and affiliates, international meeting and convention sites will grow more commonplace. While many associations handle domestic meeting coordination in-house, international meetings present more complex needs, ranging from customs to currency, and agency assistance is therefore more critical.

Car Rental

Car rental companies have long recognized the clout of associations. For most association meetings, rental cars are needed. By providing association members access to preferred pricing for association events and general rental-car usage, the rental-car company gains additional business, the member receives lower pricing, and the association often gains nondues income plus complimentary VIP cars or vans.

An association rental-car partnership can provide members with added peace of mind during travel, for the approval of the association provides members added assurance that the car will be available and that the price will be competitive. Like all other programs, if the service doesn't perform as expected, the member knows he has an added layer of recourse through the association.

Of those ASAE-member associations holding conventions during 1990–1991, for example, 21 percent named an official rental car agency, which reserved an average of 45 cars for the event.[5]

In the early 1970s the Avis Rental Car System entered the association market hoping to expand its presence in the personnel travel sector of the rental car business. Today, Avis is one of the leaders in association programs, working with hundreds of associations in the U.S., Canada, and Europe. "The key is to view the program as a partnership with the association; the member saves on car rentals and services, the association gains a member benefit and promotional support for meetings and conventions, and Avis gains a sophisticated form of niche marketing and an opportunity for incremental growth," says Jim Kraft, Avis's vice president of group sales.

Through its association member benefit programs, Avis has also developed additional services in response to the needs of the members, such as weekly and monthly rental programs. The key is to "keep the program in front of the membership; promote, promote, promote. Use every opportunity to remind the association and its member of the program and its success, including the association's new-member kits, member-usage reports, member feedback, and the presentation of royalty checks," says Kraft.

Prepaid Legal Services

Even though we are living in an increasingly complicated and litigious society, most Americans do not have a family attorney. Therefore many critical individual legal needs are often left unaddressed, such as estate planning and wills. In addition, small businesses often attempt to fend for themselves, despite an increasing regulatory burden in many businesses and the ongoing need for corporate planning, contract work, and collection assistance.

It is estimated that over 25,000 lawyers now participate in prepaid legal services and that over 17.5 million Americans now participate. These programs usually follow two formats: group discount plans, where participants receive discounts when they use lawyers or law firms recommended by the plan, prepaid access, in which a basic menu of legal services is included, while others are available at discounted fees.[6] Such programs provide the member either a source of primary assistance or an additional source of industry- or professional-specific information, such as interpreting government regulations or responding to threatened government actions or penalties.

Such services also provide the association with a turnkey method to respond to member inquiries. Most associations lack the resources to respond to individual member concerns and therefore concentrate on the broader questions facing the profession or industry. By offering prepaid legal services, an association can refer members with specific questions to a source that is experienced in the issue. In addition, the provider of the service often provides the association with an expert source of ongoing legal counsel and member education. The association therefore is able to address critical member needs, generate nondues revenue, and broaden its ability to assist members when they need it the most.

An attorney or law firm whose practice is concentrated in a specialized arena may find that associations offer a unique vehicle to expand that practice while also providing associations with a service that their members welcome.

Premiums/Incentives/Novelties

Many businesses and occupations use premiums and incentives for marketing and motivation. An association can provide a supplier of premiums a strategic partner that can target its marketing efforts and provide a reliable source of business. Remember that the association market is twofold: the association itself—for many associations will provide premiums for convention attendees or produce a wide variety of novelties that bear the association's logo and name for member sale—and the association's members, who use both premiums and novelties in their individual marketing.

The Distributive Education Clubs of America, through its 6,000 chapters, represents high school students majoring in marketing. In addition to a wide array of educational publications and programs that support entrepreneurship, the association also offers its members novelties (t-shirts, sweatshirts, cups, etc.) emblazoned with the association's name and logo to promote membership pride. The association now offers over 160 products for member purchase that are produced by various manufacturers.

THE FUTURE

While association group purchasing programs are growing rapidly, many opportunities are yet untapped. In fact, it is estimated that over 60 percent of associations offer no group purchasing programs to their members.[7] The members of trade or professional associations are buyers of every product and service marketed today, and just as warehouses and clubs have brought the advantages of bulk buying to the public, associations can provide such a "club" opportunity for products more specific to their members.

Opportunities include an expansion of bulk-purchasing programs to address a broader array of products that are specific to the member's industry and the offering of such programs with payment options catered to the memberships' needs. An area often overlooked is the provision of professional services, such as tax preparation, accounting, audit, and consulting needs. By packaging professional services to address the specific and easily defined membership needs, members will gain improved pricing and access, the association will gain a valuable and tangible member benefit, and the provider will acquire increased market share through targeted marketing.

KEYS TO SUCCESS

1. Success depends largely on your ability to design your service to the specific needs of the association's membership. Take the time to understand the association's membership and then design programs that meet the members' specific needs.

2. While price is one factor in success, consistent member communication and quality service are often deciding factors. The endorsement of an association is only the first step in the sales process, not the last. Your ultimate success will be judged to the extent that you leverage the association's communication channels with your marketing and sales activities.

3. Seek association partners that compliment your sales, product distribution, and support structures. Associations seek partners who can ensure the delivery of high quality products, maintain pricing integrity, and offer after-the-sale support. The greater the extent that a corporation controls the sale and support of its products, the greater its chances of success with associations.

4. Recognize that the association market is one built on "high touch" and relationship; be prepared for the long term—results don't come overnight. The endorsement of an association provides a critical marketing edge, but long-term success is built by one satisfied member at a time. One of the greatest tools in association program marketing is the testimonial of a satisfied member; broadcast such success stories whenever possible.

5. Build on your strengths and leverage your market knowledge—work first with associations that represent your customers and then expand to those that represent new markets or prospects. By working with associations that represent your core market, you increase your odds of early association success, which can easily be extended to other associations.

6. All too often, vendors bypass associations that represent their core markets, since they feel they already have the dominant market share. After all, if you already "own" the market, why offer an association program and possibly reduce your margins? In these competitive times retaining your market is just as important as penetrating a new market. If you ignore your core

market's association, you can be assured that your competition won't.

7. Develop a marketing plan and fully understand the communications channels available through the association. Once you have won the endorsement, take advantage of all the opportunities that it provides. It's critical that your marketing plan be developed in conjunction with the association to ensure that all available resources are harnessed.

8. Establish reasonable goals for the program and don't oversell the association. Unrealistic revenue projections will come back to haunt you. Base your projections on the association's prior experiences with other programs and with a clear understanding of the association's marketing capabilities.

9. Sell your sales force. An association program should provide your sales force with quality leads and a higher closing ratio. Involve your top sales people early in your association discussion to ensure that the program can be supported in the field and that any potential conflicts with existing customers or pricing can be addressed.

10. Keep the association informed as to both your progress and your problems. Good news needs to be broadcast and bad news needs to be managed—the association can help do both. The bottom line of a successful partnership—no surprises.

NOTES

1. American Society of Association Executives, *Policies and Procedures in Association Management*, (ASAE, 1992), p. 101.

2. Ibid.

3. Ibid.

4. American Society of Association Executives, *Association Meeting Trends 1992* (ASAE, 1992), p. xv.

5. *Association Meeting Trends*, 1992, p. x.

6. Alec Swartz, "Prepaid Legal Services: An Employee Benefit Program Option," *The John Liner Review* (Winter 1992), pp. 42–43.

7. *Policies and Procedures in Association Management*, p. 101.

Chapter Six

Insurance Programs

The ideal association program is one that attracts and retains members while building a solid source of nondues revenue. The reasons are clear. Associations are groups of people or businesses that share common needs and, from an insurance view, common underwriting characteristics. Associations represent an alternative distribution channel that can, through target marketing, increase productivity and marketing efficiency, and, with its strong membership affinity, increase persistency.

While the diversification of insurance opportunities is staggering, they generally fall into three categories: group insurance programs, property-casualty plans, and association insurance agencies. Professional associations or societies, with individuals as members, tend to emphasize group insurance, including health, dental, life, and disability coverage, and occupational liability insurance. Trade associations, with businesses as members, typically offer property-casualty coverage including liability, workman's compensation and errors and omissions, and employee benefit programs. Association insurance agencies, on the other hand, are a relatively new phenomena that have found a home within both trade and professional associations.

GROUP INSURANCE

Group insurance is a natural fit for association marketing, for associations are prefabricated groups that share common characteristics and, from a sales viewpoint, are often motivated by both peer action and belief in the association and its cause. Group insurance insurers and agents will find the association market both interested and hesitant, frequently at the same time.

While the need for alternative health insurance options has never been greater, and insurance programs are a proven membership magnet, many association remain gun-shy. For nothing can destroy the integrity of an association faster than double digit rate hikes or, worse, claims that go unpaid or members denied coverage.

A survey conducted by the American Society of Association Executives (ASAE) and W.F. Morneau and Associates found that 29 percent of associations surveyed offer health insurance plans to their members. The survey of over 2,500 associations also shows that those association programs have $6.2 billion of annual premium and cover 1.9 million people. Perhaps as impressive, the average association-provided plan covers 27 percent of the association's membership.[1] While some associations administer and market their programs, 73 percent of associations polled rely on insurance carriers and brokers to administer and market their programs, rather than utilize alternatives such as captives or self-insurance.[2]

While many national associations are currently providing some group insurance, their scope of offerings differs widely. While some associations offer a full menu of group insurance programs, many sponsor direct-mail programs that address single needs, such as hospital indemnification, accidental coverage, and disability income plans.

The American Association of Retired Persons' (AARP) group health insurance program, which is underwritten and administered by The Prudential, is likely one of the largest group accounts in America. The program, which now insures over 19 percent of AARP's 33 million members, 50 percent in the program's medicare supplement plans, and 50 percent in the hospital indemnity plan, generated $22 billion in premiums in 1991.

Prudential, which was awarded the AARP account in 1981 and today represents its largest group case, feels that the oversight and review by AARP provides members greater buying comfort and confidence, and has resulted in a lower lapse rate than experienced in other group cases. Due in part to the joint efforts of the AARP and The Prudential, participating members have received premium refunds in five of the last eight years, due to better-than-expected underwriting experience and expense

control. In 1992 alone, participating AARP members shared over
$240 million in premium refunds, a testimonial to the program's
success and a powerful membership magnet.

AARP and The Prudential are constantly seeking to introduce
health insurance products that serve the needs of the members.
Within the past few years they have begun to market long-term-
care insurance plans, and more recently, have introduced a new
Hospital Advantage Plan (HAP) for the 50 to 63 age group. HAP
is intended for members and spouses not yet eligible for medicare who have no other individual or employer coverage. HAP
also offers different rates for smokers and nonsmokers.

Commercial Life Insurance Company has served the association market since 1928 and is one of the leading providers in association disability insurance. Beginning with associations that
represented teachers, Commercial Life has expanded to professional associations that represent accounting, medical, and
dental fields. To date the company, working in conjunction with
third-party administrators, has enrolled almost 2,000 associations. The key, according to Commercial's vice president of association group sales, Ted Merrill, is to "differentiate your
product from those available 'off-the-street' through price, contract language, limits, underwriting simplicity, and ease of
issue."

Commercial Life Insurance targets professional associations
that have a minimum of 750 members, have an average age of
under 50, and have incomes in excess of $40,000 per year. Com-
mercial Life also seeks associations that have exhibited success
with previous programs, have communication channels to their
members, and have members that rely on the association for professional education and licensing.

Association marketing is credited with Commercial Life's high
penetration rate and reduced acquisition costs that can be passed
on as improved member benefits. With over 300,000 lives now
insured, Ted Merrill states that "the market has just been
scratched and more association opportunities are being uncovered every day."

Working with its 22,000 independent insurance agents and associates at the regional, state, and district levels American Family
Life Assurance of Columbus (AFLAC) is the world's leading

writer of supplemental health insurance. AFLAC markets supplemental benefit programs to more than 87,000 payroll groups in the United States and 43,000 groups in Japan. Based on its successful "clusterselling", where businesses are approached and premiums are paid through payroll deduction, AFLAC now works with hundreds of associations, both trade and professional.

With a broad menu of programs, including hospital-intensive care, hospital indemnity, cancer insurance, accident and disability insurance, and long-term-care and medicare supplements, AFLAC can design affinity programs to suit most memberships. AFLAC has found that associations with individual members can be effectively marketed both intensive care and hospital indemnity via direct mail, while the members of trade associations and their employees are best targeted through the one-on-one efforts of its sales force.

According to Edith Kaiser, AFLAC's account executive for affinity groups, "Members are increasingly receptive to supplemental benefits because of both their guaranteed renewability feature and the lack of rate volatility often experienced in group health insurance programs. It seems that people today are not as concerned with the inevitability of death but with the ever-increasing cost of maintaining their health."

To support its association marketing, AFLAC appoints, for each association, a special projects coordinator in each state who is responsible for implementing the program according to the explicit guidelines approved by each association. In addition, AFLAC's field force is encouraged to refer affinity leads to the home office for follow-up and assistance in program negotiation to ensure that all members, regardless of their location, can be served.

Edith Kaiser believes that the future of association marketing is strong. "As members recognize the increased cost of health care and associations seek nondues income, supplemental benefits make a perfect fit—the association is able to offer a program with high member acceptance while the members gain access to affordably priced products."

With the average cost of health insurance approaching $4,000 per employee per year, it is one of the largest expenses that small businesses face. The process of buying group insurance, often viewed on par with a root canal, is complex, time-consuming, and painful.[3] Association programs often can provide small businesses and professionals alternative programs that can leverage the collective needs of the association's membership. Association programs can often provide increased options, carrier stability, and the advantage of pooled claim experience which enables risk to be diffused among the association's participating members, thus reducing premium volatility.

PROPERTY-CASUALTY PROGRAMS

Today 17 percent of associations with budgets over $500,000 provide some type of property-casualty insurance program to their members. According to a survey conducted by the ASAE and The Aon Specialty Group, coverage most commonly offered in conjunction with a commercial carrier include: worker's compensation 61 percent, property (fire) 56 percent, general and automobile liability 54 percent and 48 percent respectively, umbrella liability 42 percent, crime 32 percent, errors and omissions 22 percent, and directors and officers 21 percent. While some programs are offered through risk-retention groups, purchasing groups, self-insurance pools and captive insurance companies, 86 percent of programs are offered through commercial insurance carriers, managing general agents, and brokers.[4]

It is interesting to note the premium volume distribution of these programs and the dominance of liability programs. Worker's compensation generated 34 percent of surveyed volume, followed by errors and omissions programs; 24 percent, general liability 13 percent, and directors and officers 8 percent. The remaining coverage—crime, property, automobile, and umbrella—generated only 22 percent of the property-casualty premium combined. The distribution reflects one of the keys to association success—target associations and develop programs that address member problems. For while crime, property, automobile, and umbrella coverage are generally available for most businesses, many businesses and professionals are faced with limited options for liability protection.[5]

According to the survey by the ASAE and the Aon Specialty Group, associations that sponsor or endorse a commercial carrier's program usually share the need for specialized policy forms, marketing expertise, program income, have member operations that are homogeneous, have a conservative philosophy, and lack the capitalization funds necessary for a captive.[6]

These association programs are finding a receptive audience and are generating impressive premium volumes. The same survey found that the average participation rate among members is over 33 percent and the average program generates $7 million in annual premiums. The marketing success is also providing associations a reliable source of nondues income, and, in more than 45 percent of the programs, also providing remuneration to the association's members, most commonly in the form of dividends based on underwriting results.[7]

The St. Paul Fire and Marine Insurance Company, the nation's 16th largest property–liability insurer, sells insurance and insurance-related services through a network of independent insurance agents in the United States and Canada. One of the niche marketing strategies employed by the St. Paul is association sponsorship, especially where the association compliments a target insurance market such as financial services, professional liability, and medical services. (See Exhibit 6–1.)

The St. Paul has found that associations that support programs promoting loss control, risk management, and marketing, especially through the provision of a dividend plan for participants, are the most likely to succeed. An effective program not only increases market share but, as importantly, can improve retention in soft and competitive markets.

When Royal Insurance developed its strategic direction for the 1990s, one key strategy involved focusing on the association and affinity-group business. While Royal had targeted commercial groups for over 20 years, it established a dedicated association unit, National Program Operations (NPO), in 1990. The unit concentrates on national associations capable of producing $5 million in annual premiums and that have an average account size of at least $25,000. NPO has grown from a staff of 30 to a staff of 180 and its 21 programs generated over $130 million in business in 1992.

EXHIBIT 6–1
Setting Your Sights

Thinking of including some target markets in your book of business? Here are some market and coverage considerations as you begin to set your sights on what could prove to be profitable niches:

Market

- Strength in numbers: Does the target market offer a reasonable potential base of customers? Business chains might be a place to start your thinking.
- Sponsorships: Are the members of the target market represented by a trade association? Obtaining the "stamp of approval" from associations for your program may help generate business.
- Location, location, location: Consider the location of the customers. Some target groups are concentrated in specific regions, while others operate nationally.
- Consistency: Do the target customers have relatively similar business organizations and insurance needs? The more consistency they offer, the better the change to establish a program that meets their needs.
- Opportunity: Your chances of success increase when you concentrate on trade groups where the competition may not be overwhelming. Sometimes, a market perceived by the competition as a less-than-optimal risk group offers opportunity.

Coverage

- Programs: Take advantage of programs already being offered by The St. Paul for target markets.
- Enhance: Would any enhancements of existing coverage better serve the customers' needs? Sometimes relatively minor changes in coverage can create a much better "fit" with the business you're targeting.
- Modify: Does the target market have unique insurance needs that can be satisfied by altering an existing coverage?
- Create: Perhaps the insurance industry does not even offer a coverage specifically aimed at the target market. Get in on the ground floor with the creation of a brand new coverage.
- Rating/Pricing: The business of some target markets doesn't lend itself to standard rating and pricing practices. A new slant on either rating or pricing might be the key to establishing a niche.
- Services/Marketing: New applications of claim or risk management services (or new services) can open the eyes of potential customers to the value-added benefits of insuring with The St. Paul.

St. Paul Fire and Marine Insurance Company, © 1991. Reprinted with permission.

Royal Insurance also recognized the potential of state and regional associations, which are marketed through its local branch offices. These affinity-group marketing programs are targeted at groups that exhibit three key criteria: the sponsoring association must have a strong and ongoing relationship with its members, members must have confidence and trust in the association, and that trust must enable the association to exert a strong influence on the buying decisions of the members. Recognizing that state and regional associations have fewer members, Royal only requires that they be capable of generating $1 million of premium within three years.

Eugene Rafter, new program manager of Royal's National Program Operations, states that "there are plenty of opportunities for producers to identify association prospects—referrals from satisfied clients, hobbies, professional affiliation, or social activities. The field force quickly finds that it's easier to attract and retain business through association programs—and that's the bottom line for us and the producer."

Royal also supports its broker and producer prospecting by exhibiting at the conventions of association executives and advertising in the trade magazines that association executives read (see Exhibit 6–2).

ASSOCIATION AGENCIES

Due in part to the success of association insurance programs, some associations have formed insurance agencies. These agencies, typically for-profit subsidiaries, permit the association to take a more active marketing role and generate additional income. An association insurance agency provides the association a vehicle to market critical coverage and ensure the delivery of high quality service through agents who understand the association and its members' needs. In the ASAE/Aon Specialty Group survey, of the 922 associations which responded, 15 percent had association-owned agencies.[8] These agencies can provide the insurance carrier with a viable and active insurance marketing channel, with critical access to the association's membership.

EXHIBIT 6–2
Royal Insurance Association Advertisement

While some of these agencies are start-ups, other associations seek out existing agencies on which to build an association division or partnership. Associations often find that existing agencies provide the association a vehicle to offer a full menu of services, with only minimal start-up capital and limited goodwill risk. Associations typically judge prospective agencies by their insurance expertise, carrier access, and membership awareness. Often, association partnerships can offer agencies an additional marketing channel that can compliment their core business, while the association gains a vehicle to enhance membership through the delivery of insurance services developed to meet the membership's needs.

INSURANCE PROGRAM DEVELOPMENT

As you begin to explore the potential of association delivery, consider the 3 m's—membership, market, and management:

Membership

1. Who are the association's members and how available is membership data? Remember that many associations represent broader industries; if you are selling a product to a specialized group within a larger industry, your results will be improved and your marketing more targeted by focusing on an association that represents only that specialty.

Associations, like companies, have different membership records and data bases. The greater the detail available regarding the membership, the easier the feasibility study becomes.

2. How many current members are there and how many eligible nonmembers are there? Insurance is a game of numbers and successful programs need a reasonable base on which to prospect. Since many associations use insurance programs as a prospecting tool for nonmembers, the potential audience is as important as the current members.

3. Where are the members? While some associations represent members nationwide, others represent state or local memberships; your target associations are ones that best fit your

capability to sell and service. This question should encompass a review of your licensing limits, your sales force distribution and support, and your ability to monitor support and claims administration.

4. What are the membership's "hot-buttons"? Many an association program has been born out of crisis. Members in need often call upon their association to help. Programs that are developed to solve member needs will succeed far more than those developed solely to generate association income.

5. What is the relationship between the association and its chapters or affiliates? It is critical that a company understand the politics of the state and national relationship. The ideal relationship is one in which the local affiliates support a larger program; however, in some associations, the relationship between the national and local chapters is competitive and marketing therefore more challenging.

The Market

1. What is the competition? Determine where members buy the coverage now and the stability of the market. A membership that is shopping for an alternative is a motivated market that is ready for a change. In addition many associations consider insurance programs in order to differentiate themselves from other associations or to compete against them. Become aware of associations that compete against your targeted association and what programs they are now offering.

2. Where does your company want to be? If your company is seeking to capture an increasing share of its existing book of business, then focus on associations that your customers belong to. On the other hand, if your company is seeking to enter a new market, use an association program as a vehicle to target your marketing.

Management

1. The association's management. Does the association appear to have the communication channels and commitment necessary for the program's success? Insurance programs need to be kept

in front of the membership, and associations with conventions, magazines, newsletters, and other ongoing marketing or communication channels are able to provide the critical support needed.

2. Your company management. Does your company have the capability and commitment to market and deliver insurance programs through an alternative distribution channel? Association programs have a long berthing process and success does not come overnight. Your company must recognize the long-term nature of the market and have the sales force and service staff to support its demands.

INSURANCE PROSPECTING

Without question the key to prospecting in the association market is to make sure your eyes and ears—the sales force—are aware of your interest and of what constitutes an association prospect.

One option is to provide your sales force with a questionnaire that sales people can use to help identify association prospects and determine if the association meets the company's underwriting criteria. These surveys usually seek information on the association, demographics of the membership, existing insurance programs, attitudes toward the current program, membership's affinity with the association, and the association's hot-buttons. It is that last item—hot-buttons—that is perhaps the most important. The single largest factor in selling associations is whether or not the program is viewed as helping to solve a problem. The hotter the problem, the hotter your association prospect.

One of the easiest methods of prospecting for association candidates is to know your desired market and keep abreast of its challenges. Each time that an industry or profession is in the news, it's likely that an insurance opportunity has been uncovered. The time to contact an association prospect is when the problem is uppermost in the association's concerns. Remember that opportunities go beyond an industry or profession being unable to purchase coverage; often associations also face insurance needs when their members confront new liabilities or regulations or provide new or expanded products or services. Keeping up with your top association prospects may be easier than you think:

• Subscribe to the association's magazine or newsletter. Each issue usually addresses the key concern of the association, new regulations and liabilities and new industry challenges.

• Join the association as a corporate member. This membership normally provides the corporation with the association magazine, newsletter and limited marketing access, such as trade show attendance and direct mail privileges.

• Exhibit at the association's trade show and make a special attempt to talk with members regarding their insurance coverage and issues related to rates and renewal problems.

• Interview your existing clients. They may already belong to some of your prospective associations and may provide you with an inside view of the association and the members problems. Referrals to an association from satisfied customers and members are your best door-openers.

• Keep your ear to the street. Associations with insurance programs often are willing to entertain competitive bids upon renewal. These associations are often excellent targets since they have membership data, marketing experience, and, often, underwriting data.

• Know their competition. If one association has an insurance program, find out who their competing association is. Often an association will seek to offer an insurance program in response to the actions of a competing association, both to retain members and to neutralize the competing association's new membership weapon.

INSURANCE PROGRAM "INSIDE" CRITERIA

Associations view the adoption of an insurance program to be one of their most important decisions. The right program can bring the association satisfied members, new recruits, nondues income, and often a enhance image among its members. However, it is the nightmare of a poor program that haunts many an executive and drives his cautious evaluation. Generally associations will judge insurance proposals by the following criteria:

• Association involvement. Most associations do not wish to assume risk, but most want to be involved in the program and receive information on which to judge an insurance company's marketing and underwriting experience. Many association will seek information such as loss statistics, premium income, insurer profit and expenses, and member participation. The greater the information, the greater the program will be viewed by the association as a partnership.

• Member service. Associations want to provide member services that are able to attract and retain members. A well-designed insurance program is a proven member service. Generally association insurance programs are judged by the degree that they: provide coverage that would be unavailable to nonmembers, ensure members a more stable market, provide broader or more specialized coverage than available outside of the program, and provide an economic incentive, such as lower price, dividend, or profit participation.[9]

• Revenue. While member service is usually the driving force, the program's compensation is also a significant consideration. Remember that there are two revenue streams: one to the association and one to participating members. The association usually receives royalties based on the program's premium volume, while the member often receives a dividend based on loss control. Association programs have proven to reduce program losses due to the association's ability to assist in communicating loss-prevention-program information and initiatives. The insurer wins through lower loss ratios and the members benefit through dividends.

• Carrier strength. An association's worst fear is an insurance carrier unable to support the program's marketing, premium volume, or losses. Most associations will require that an insurer have a best rating of no less than "A." In addition to financial strength, often the most important insurance company characteristic is its reputation, especially its track record of member service. A carrier who has a reputation of supporting and then abandoning a market will find associations difficult to penetrate.

• Coverage. Associations generally prefer to offer coverage designed to meet their specific member needs, rather than endorse an off-the-shelf policy.[10] Policies designed with the member in mind usually provide customized coverage or policy limits that meet most of the member needs.

• Relationship with agent/broker. Associations look for agents and brokers with a proven track record of working with associations and, ideally, their members. Often associations seek financial data on the agent or broker to ensure that they have the staying power to support the program's marketing and administration. Many associations are also concerned about the agents or brokers intent to cross-sell other nonendorsed products or products that may conflict with another association program.

• Member access. While few insurance programs will accept all applicants, an association program needs to ensure that it meets the needs and is accessible by the majority of members. Testing the program's application and underwriting criteria with association focus groups can often overcome association hesitation.

• Marketing. Associations will generally rely on the insurance carrier or agent to market the program. Program proposals are often judged by the extent to which they detail a marketing plan that encompasses the association's communication tools and utilizes the insurers or agent's marketing resources.

THE FUTURE

As insurance companies continue to seek more economical ways to deliver insurance products and services and consumers gain confidence in receiving advice and purchasing programs by mail, the value of association partnerships will certainly increase. Edgar W. Armstrong, managing director of risk management services for Aon Specialty Group, insurance consultants and actuaries to many affinity groups, states, "Affinity marketing is the wave of the future. One-on-one marketing is just too expensive. Frankly, it's one of only effective ways to compete against 'direct writers'."

While many of the larger associations have insurance programs in place, one of the growing opportunities is the replacement of inadequate or marginal programs by carriers and agents with both financial and marketing stamina. In addition while many companies have called on the leading associations, many second tier, smaller national, state, and local associations have been overlooked. "Association partnerships enable insurance companies to access markets with the credibility of the association," says Edgar Armstrong. "These days there are few new products; the key therefore, is how a company packages and markets its products."

INSURANCE PROGRAMS—KEYS TO SUCCESS

Despite a track record of long-term success, many association programs fail. The reasons for failure are the lessons for program success:

1. Remember that there are few programs that can destroy an association's good name faster than an insurance program that does not deliver as promised. While a successful insurance program is a proven winner for both nondues income and membership retention, it is also the one that associations fear the most. Before you sell your product or program, sell your company and your commitment; if you can't win the association's confidence, you won't win the sale.

2. Recognize the long-term commitment necessary for success. While the endorsement of an association provides a valuable door-opener, it should only be the first step in a coordinated marketing plan. The success of an association program is often judged more by its staying power than by its pricing at any one time. Those agents and insurers who judge the association market after a short time frame will likely be disappointed and, more importantly, overlook the long-term rewards.

3. Set realistic goals for the program. Many failures are successes that were simply overestimated. In conjunction with the association, examine the market, the competition, and the interest level, then establish mutual goals that can guide your marketing efforts. Without realistic mutual goals, one party may

view the program as a success and the other view it as a failure; but in either case, the program's marketing and support will suffer.

4. Know the association. Too often, an insurance company will select an association based on limited information and simply assume it represents the company's target market. Remember that many associations represent an industry or occupation; take the time to locate the ones that are both capable and motivated.

If your prospective partner is a national association, determine what the relationship between the association and its state or local affiliates is. The ideal program is one that can be supported at both national and local levels, rather than a program that faces competition from the association's affiliates.

5. Test the water first. Membership surveys can be a very effective tool to wed the association to your program and determine membership interest in program development. Often associations can also assist by sponsoring focus groups to test program blueprints.

6. Keep the association informed of problems and progress. The more you treat the association as a partner, rather than simply an endorser, the greater the odds of the program's success. Remember that the association's reputation is on the line; satisfied members are the key to marketing and dissatisfied members need to be managed. An informed association partner can help you sell a rate hike or a claim-paying problem. An uninformed association, when confronted with surprise problems, can become your worst enemy.

7. Always sell. While the hard-sell should be avoided at all costs, your program should be sold at every opportunity—keep it in front of the member. Announce program milestones, broadcast new member participants, and mail announcements of program enhancements and even additions to your sales force due to the program's success.

8. Involve your whole organization. Nothing is more frustrating to an association than a member that calls for program information and finds that no one has heard of the program or knows whom to talk to. Unfortunately this happens all too often, and countless opportunities are wasted. The key is to involve your whole organization in the program, from the receptionist to the underwriters, the sales force and the marketing division.

The more your organization can talk like the association, the more welcome members will feel. Consider mailing the association's magazine or newsletter to your sales force and home office personnel; the gesture will permit your staff to understand the issues that the membership is facing and talk their language.

9. Solve problems. The best programs are born out of crisis. Read the newspaper and focus on industries facing price volatility or access problems; the association will be more receptive and the membership more responsive. Regardless of the program, sell answers not problems, for members are looking for solutions. How does the program simplify decision making, increase coverage, and increase member confidence?

10. Consider limited offers or open seasons. Association members, like most of us, would rather not change their insurance plans. Often by offering a reason to act now, the association program can be "kick-started." Consider open seasons, but keep the open window to less than 90 days, and focus it around the buying season or an association event such as the convention. The offer permits you and the association to concentrate your marketing during a limited period.

INSURANCE OPPORTUNITIES INTERVIEW WORK SHEET
The survey is not product specific (property-casualty, group health, group disability or personal lines programs) therefore questions should be modified to elicit more specific membership or underwriting data.

Name _____   Title _____

Association _____   Phone# _____ Fax# _____

Association Membership Profile

What is the mission of the association:

_____

_____

Number of members: Companies _____ Individuals _____

Location of members: national, state or regional? If national, are they concentrated in one or more areas?

_____

Member information: Information that is relevant to the type of insurance being researched (average number of employees, revenues of businesses, similarity of businesses).

_____

Association Insurance Experience

Does the association now offer any association insurance programs to its members? If so, what coverage is provided and what percentage of the membership participates?

_____

Has the association sponsored or offered insurance programs previously that are no longer being marketed, if so, why were they discontinued (lack of volume, loss ratios, premium payment practices)?

_____

Does the association have an insurance agency, captive, or association subsidiary that markets or manages the programs for the association?

_____

What areas could be improved in your current insurance program support (marketing, administration, claims paying, problem resolution, policy competitiveness, coverage, underwriting attitudes, etc)?

_____

For sponsored programs, when does your current contract expire and what is the process for evaluation and negotiation.

_____

_____

Member Insurance Needs

Do you feel the insurance needs of your membership are currently being met?

_____

Have you received any inquiries from members seeking insurance coverage? If so, for what risks?

_____

Are there any trends, new technologies, or government regulations that may affect your members' insurance needs?

_____

Are there any coverages or services that your members need that are particularly difficult to obtain? If so, why?

_____

_____

Association Marketing Capability

What methods of communication with membership does the association use that might be utilized to advise members of insurance programs or services?

_____ Magazine (frequency _____)

_____ Newsletter (frequency _____)

_____ Conventions (frequency/next _____)

_____ Trade show (frequency/next show _____)

Other association communication vehicles

Does the association have any state chapters or local affiliates? What is their relationship with your association and the services it supports?
Do any of your chapters or affiliates now offer insurance programs to their members?

Wrap-Up

What is your association decision-making process? If the process involves a committee, when does the committee meet next?

(If the association meets your basic criteria) Would the association be interested in conducting a joint survey of its members to determine if their insurance needs are being met?

What is our next step?

Request information to assist your further research: association's annual report, magazine media kit, membership kit

NOTES

1. "Survey Studies Association-provided Insurance" *Association Management* (January 1993), p. 7.
2. American Society of Association Executives, *Policies and Procedures in Association Management* (ASAE, 1992), p. 93.
3. Roger Thompson, "How to Buy Health Insurance," *Nation's Business* (October 1992), p. 16.
4. American Society of Association Executives and Aon Specialty Group, *The Association Insurance Program Guide & Survey Report* (ASAE, 1993), p. 82.
5. Ibid., p. 83.
6. Ibid., p. 50.
7. Ibid., p. 76.
8. Ibid., p. 57.
9. Edgar Armstrong, "Does Your Sponsored Insurance Program Measure Up?", *Association Management* (December 1988), p. 56.
10. Ibid., p. 57.

Chapter Seven

Financial Services Opportunities

The success of insurance programs and the alternative distribution capability of financial companies is generating an accelerating interest in association partnerships. Today virtually any product that can be delivered through a bank can be delivered through an association program. Associations offer financial service providers a method to reach their targeted audience and increase marketing results, often while reducing expenses.

Although still in their infancy, association partnerships are offering financial services including credit cards, cash management services, pension programs, loan programs, mutual funds, and even mortgage loans. The key is to design a program that recognizes the unique needs of the association's membership. The more customized the program, the greater the success.

THE PIONEER: CREDIT CARDS

One of the first efforts to tap the marketing leverage of associations was credit card programs. Affinity card programs, which allow association members to obtain credit cards through their association membership, began in the late 1970s as banks sought new ways of attracting credit card accounts. Credit card providers recognized the need to explore alternative marketing channels that could deliver higher response rates and therefore lower acquisition costs. The association market offered a vehicle by which credit card marketing could be targeted to specific professions and occupations, who share purchasing habits, credit card usage patterns, and credit worthiness.

Visa International, the world's largest consumer card payment system, reports that more than 2,750 Visa affinity card programs have been launched worldwide, many with associations and other nonprofit groups such as colleges and universities. To date it has been estimated that over 25 million affinity cards have been issued—over 10 percent of all the credit cards in America.[1] The success story of affinity credit cards is a valuable lesson in the development of other association financial services (see Exhibit 7–1).

The Bank

Lower cardholder acquisition costs and lower cardholder turnover. It has been estimated that the average marketing cost to acquire a new credit card customer is $75. Affinity marketing has proved to reduce marketing costs through higher response and renewal rates due to members' beliefs in the association and its cause.

Improved credit experience. Affinity credit cards have generally experienced fewer credit problems than nonaffinity cards, although experience differs among associations. Certainly part of this improved performance is due to the ability of banks to target desirable occupations or professions, rather than rely on mass mailing.

Increased market share. Associations provide a vehicle to market credit cards to selected markets with the clout of the association. MBNA of America Bank, for example, doesn't rely on mass-mailed solicitations, but has nevertheless issued cards to one-third of all doctors and one-fifth of all lawyers in the country by obtaining the endorsement of their organizations and associations.[2]

Added revenue. Although the bank usually pays a royalty to the association based on the cards issued, the credit card issuer gains through increased card usage. A survey of the *American Banker* found that 45 percent of Americans would use their

EXHIBIT 7–1
Affinity Credit Card "Mock-Ups"

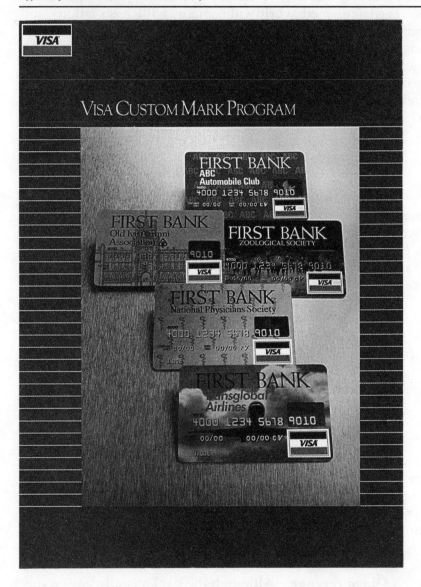

Used with the permission of Visa International.

affinity card before their nonaffinity card, and other studies have found that consumers spend 20 percent more on affinity credit cards than on standard cards—a testimonial to member loyalty.[3]

Cross-sell opportunities. Once an association member is a satisfied cardholder, he is often receptive to other products offered by the financial institution, such as credit lines, home equity loans, and retirement accounts.

The Association

Visibility is increased. Affinity credit cards usually carry the name or logo of the sponsoring association on the front of the card. Each time a member makes a purchase, he is reminded of the association and experiences a tangible membership benefit. In addition, since many credit card companies use telemarketing to solicit members, the association's name receives additional exposure.

Membership value is increased. An affinity card is viewed as a valuable member benefit that the member sees each time he makes a purchase. Often the affinity card offers group members special perks or discounts associated with membership in the organization, which increases card value and usage.

Nondues income. To recognize the value of the association's name, goodwill, and logo, financial institutions usually pay royalties to the association. Royalties are paid to the association to supplement the need for dues income or are designated for specific causes. Consumers who carry the National Audubon Society Visa affinity credit card, for example, trigger a donation to the organization each time the card is used for purchases. In 1991 alone, the Audubon Society received approximately $100,000 from the use of its 10,000 cards.[4]

Communication increases. Each month that the members of the association receive a credit card statement, they receive a reminder of their association and often messages or other services from the association.

Dues collection. Associations, particularly professional groups and societies, can collect membership dues by billing their members' accounts; this can increase renewals and the association's investment float.

The Member

Pride and increased awareness of membership. Each time a member uses the association's card, he is able to demonstrate support for the association and is reminded of the value of his membership. Members also view the revenue that their card usage generates for the association as additional support of the association and as a way of reducing future dues increases. Preferred pricing/benefits-affinity credit card programs often offer members lower interest rates and/or annual fees than are easily available to nonmembers. Since the cards are targeted to specified groups, special promotions and other benefits may be tied to card usage.

Based on the success of affinity credit cards, some banks are now teaming up with corporations. Cobranded credit cards combine the brand names of large corporations with bank issuers in order to target the customer base of the corporation. Cobranded cards are founded on the assumption that consumers will spend more when their credit card is tied to discounts or access to specific products or services. Since 1990, almost 100 different cobranded card programs have been launched with such corporate giants as General Motors, General Electric, and American Telephone and Telegraph.[5]

It is too early to tell whether consumers will feel as strongly about a corporation's products as they do about an association or charity that they have chosen to join.

The Future

While some view the affinity credit card market as saturated, it is important to note that as a product evolves, the potential affinity-related benefits also expand. The credit card has changed rapidly from simply an American way of paying for goods to an internationally-accepted currency. According to Visa International, affinity card programs are now in operation in the United Kingdom, Belgium, the Netherlands, and Spain. In 1992 the trade publication, *Cards International*, reported that a new affinity card program was being launched in Japan on a daily basis. Therefore it is likely that associations with international memberships and associations based in foreign countries will become the next hot spots for affinity cards.[6]

The growth of business card programs designed to enable businesses to provide employees with credit cards for business expenses may provide an affinity card entry vehicle for the generally untapped trade association market. In addition, the proliferation of the debit cards (where purchases are made using a card that resembles a credit card but are automatically deducted from a checking account) may open the door for affinity debit cards directed at individuals overlooked for credit cards.

While the issuance of credit cards has been the historical target of affinity programs, the processing of credit cards for businesses has become a growing focus of association marketing. For each time that a consumer makes a purchase, the business must process the transaction to ensure that payment is received. Today many trade associations that represent those members are aggregating their processing needs and negotiating lower transaction fees for their members. As the processing of credit cards continues to move from paper-based to electronic, the role of trade associations will likely increase as their members seek economic access to both the equipment and the processing of transactions.

MUTUAL FUNDS

With the solid track record of association credit card partnerships, it is not surprising that other financial services are testing the association waters. Within the past five years, several associations have begun to offer mutual funds to their members, usually in conjunction with mutual fund groups or money managers.

The logic of investing by association is inescapable; the investors in any particular mutual fund often share common

objectives, risk tolerance, financial capabilities, and sophistica-
tion. Such are the traits often found within any group of businesses or individuals who share a common vocation, occupation,
or lifestyle. The key is obviously to determine the investment
characteristics of particular mutual fund buyers and target associations that represent the targeted groups.

Since 1984 the American Association of Retired Persons
(AARP) has sponsored mutual funds that are offered in conjunction with the investment firm of Scudder, Stevens, and Clark.
Today, the eight funds, customized for the association's membership, have over $8 billion in assets, with the majority invested
in funds viewed as "safe"—fixed-income funds. The investment
concentration is not surprising, considering the profile—over age
50—and the likely investment concerns—retirement and safety—
of the AARP's membership.[7]

The recent trend of mutual fund specialization and sector investing lends further merit to association partnering. For as
mutual funds are developed to invest in companies that are committed to specific social causes, such as clean water, recycling,
pollution control, and social responsibility, there is likely an association that advocates just such a position. Association partnering could permit members not only to voice their convictions
but also to invest in companies dedicated to addressing the
problem.

Today many regional mutual funds invest only in companies
that are located within certain states or regions. Such funds may
find a partner in associations that represent members in just
those states. The members' investment in the funds could be
viewed as a way to encourage economic development and support their market areas.

One caution for mutual funds seeking association partners is
to be sensitive to the beliefs of the group and to any potential
conflicts of interest. For example, members of a group that advocate strong drunk-driving penalties may not wish to invest in
firms involved in the liquor business. On the other hand, an association may not feel comfortable sponsoring a mutual fund
that invests in companies that may benefit or be harmed by the
association's policies or lobbying.

PENSION AND RETIREMENT PROGRAMS

Both businesses and individuals share a need for pension or retirement investment planning. Since association members are often small employers or self-employed professionals, they often lack the time and expertise to explore various retirement plans and investment options. Unfortunately, their relatively small investment potential also limits their options and the relative interest levels of sales people.

Some companies have begun to tap the association market by targeting members with retirement plans tailored for their specific needs. Some firms with retirement-planning expertise have targeted associations that represent self-employed members and are marketing tax-qualified plans, including profit sharing, 401k, pension, and defined-benefit plans.

One of the leaders in providing retirement program services to associations is The Equitable Life Assurance Society, which has targeted the association members for almost 25 years. Today the Equitable has 25,000 participating association members and over $1 billion under management. Through the Association Members Retirement Program, Equitable offers association members an array of no-load investment options, full-service plan administration, and competitive fees not easily available on an individual basis. The Equitable provides associations turnkey marketing assistance and nondues income based on participation and aggregate assets under management.

The Equitable targets associations with at least 5,000 members composed of self-employed individuals and small businesses. The ideal association membership includes members who are over the age of 40 and who generate incomes in excess of $60,000 annually. According to Jeffrey Lang, account executive of the Association Members Retirement Program, "Associations offer the opportunity to reduce marketing costs and have proven to attract higher response rates, retention, and persistency than plans sold without such an affinity." One of the keys to Equitable's success is the use of an association survey, conducted without cost to the association, to determine member interest, confirm member demographic data, and test the strength of the association's affinity.

HOME MORTGAGES

The largest investment most Americans will make is their home. Increasingly, mortgage companies are examining the potential of marketing mortgage services in partnership with associations. While historically the majority of mortgages were originated with the assistance of real estate agents, increasingly the life-blood of mortgage companies is mortgage refinancing, where individuals are often left to fend for themselves.

Whether a new mortgage or a refinance is at issue, associations represent individuals who share common characteristics that can improve mortgage marketing. For example, local and state associations may enable a lender to target states with growing economies or higher priced homes, while associations representing the military might be able to target veterans administration loans, and associations with high earning professions might be targets for jumbo loans.

The evolution of association mortgage partnerships has been accelerated by a number of factors, including the ability of mortgage companies to originate mortgage loans from a central facility, the increasing usage of fax and overnight mail, and the increasing consumer awareness of the need to shop for a mortgage loan. After all, if an association is viewed by its member as saving one-fourth of a point on the mortgage's interest rate or points, the benefit will be viewed as "paying" for the member's dues.

Based on its experience in building corporate relationships, including relocation and leasing, PHH US Mortgage, the mortgage arm of PHH Corporation, now provides centralized mortgage services to over 200 affinity groups. In the short term, Bob Nagel, president of PHH U.S Mortgage, admits that "affinity marketing is more costly, but for companies with the financial stamina, the long-term results can provide better quality leads, geographic diversity, and a reliable origination network of motivated members."

PHH US Mortgage has found that the most successful programs are those that support the mission of the association or group, assign an internal advocate for the program, and understand the long-term nature of a successful relationship. Today, affinity marketing is the fastest-growing segment of PHH US

Mortgage, which also relies on relocation and real-estate brokers to generate business.

"We believe the market has just been scratched," says president Bob Nagel. "With the increasing willingness and comfort of the American people to purchase by telephone, we can make complex products convenient. Through the use of toll-free numbers, overnight mail, and fax, customers can obtain a mortgage loan in the privacy of their home or office and at their convenience."

CASH MANAGEMENT

Recently the American Society of Association Executives developed a program with the investment firm of Legg Mason that offers associations various investment services, including the management of operating funds, pension funds, and foundation money. The program also offers associations cash management alternatives, including certificates of deposit shopping, mutual funds, and professionally managed fixed-income and equity accounts.

Legg Mason's Association Investment Program recognizes that most associations, due to their small size, often have limited investment options and expertise. Using its experience in providing investment services to foundations and trust funds, Legg Mason is seeking to expand its services to associations which have historically been very conservative, driven by short-term boards of directors, and faced with the investment of long-term funds. Michael Graham, director of the investment program for Legg Mason, states that "increasingly associations are demanding that their investments work harder; after all, a better investment return is often a new-found source of nondues income."

To differentiate the program from those of other brokers, associations are offered complimentary assistance in developing written investment policies that provide the association and its board a well-documented program for satisfying its fiduciary obligations. In addition, Legg Mason has established a dedicated association fixed-income trading desk, and only brokers who understand the long-term nature of the relationship prospect for the association's clients.

Legg Mason's Michael Graham says, "While the initial response has been excellent, we recognize that we are building a long-term relationship, and our success will be built one association at a time."

MEMBER LOAN PROGRAMS

Association members represent an alternative origination network for loans. Through associations, several banks and finance companies now offer members loan programs that are customized for the particular industry or occupation. Depending on the association, loan programs may include lines of credit, equity loans, financing for equipment or inventory, or financing for the start-up or acquisition of a business or professional practice.

Member loan programs can often provide a service that goes right to the heart of an association—membership. After all, if an association's members can't sell their businesses and potential members can't raise the capital to enter the business, membership will suffer. A well-designed member loan program can provide the membership with an alternative financing source, the association with a source of nondues income, and a method to fill the membership pipeline.

THE FUTURE

As financial service providers continue to explore alternative distribution channels and as consumers become increasingly comfortable in purchasing financial services, not simply from across the street but from across the country, association partnerships will certainly grow. As one considers the broad array of financial services that can now be delivered by mail, the possibilities abound.

Professional associations could, for example, provide a vehicle to market annuities and products that fund specific needs, such as education and retirement, while trade associations may provide a conduit to deliver programs that help smaller businesses access capital markets; for while larger businesses increasingly rely on Wall Street for capital and funding, smaller businesses are often effectively barred due to the small size of their individual needs. Therefore, companies will likely find a receptive market for programs designed to improve the capital access of smaller businesses, perhaps through investment pools that aggregate the needs of many businesses and provide investors an improved spread of risk.

FINANCIAL SERVICES—KEYS TO SUCCESS

1. Know the members' needs. While many associations may know their members' purchasing habits or insurance needs, it is unlikely that many associations recognize their members' financial service concerns. Consider a joint survey with your prospective associations to uncover concerns, provide invaluable marketing assistance, and, more importantly, wed the association to you while the survey is being conducted and the results evaluated.

2. Keep it simple. To most people financial services are a foreign language they would rather not learn. Members look to an association to demystify problems and offer solutions tailored to their needs. Unlike in group purchasing, price in financial services is usually not the prime consideration; often the sale hinges on the product offering less "red tape," simplified applications, and options customized for the targeted market.

3. You can't be everything to everybody. Start your program with a core product and expand as interest and demand increases. Programs often fail to deliver expected results because members become confused with the variety of choices. When confused, the easiest course of action for the member is to do nothing.

4. Differentiate your product. Determine the "hot button" of the members or the mission of the association and build it into your product or service. For example, if the association supports a foundation or educational scholarship, you may want to design the program so that a donation is made based on sales or usage.

5. Build in features that cater to your market. If, for example, your target association represents teachers, you may want to offer the option for suspension of their program payments during their summer vacations or simply permit members to suspend payments for a month during the year. Each special feature signals your knowledge of the association and the needs of the members.

6. Sell your communication capability. An association has limited methods of reaching the membership; the monthly billing or quarterly statements of many financial services provide the association an additional vehicle for communicating with its members. Offer the association the opportunity to include notices or reminders of association events and other services in your statements or mailings. The effort also continually reminds the members of the ongoing mutual nature of the program.

7. Provide continuing education and information. Regardless of the program, by providing education and information and not simply selling a service, members will quickly differentiate your program from others currently available.

8. Keep the association involved. When the deal is signed, the program has just begun. Your goal is to make the association a proud advocate for your program. Keep the association informed of your marketing success, your enrollments, and, yes, your problems. Keep the program a partnership and both parties will work for its success. The bottom line—no surprises.

9. Testimonials sell. Association members want to know if the product works and how it has helped other members. One of the most effective tools in financial services marketing is the testimonial of satisfied customers. Testimonials can be used in advertising, direct mail, sales calls, and telemarketing to relate to other association members.

10. Sell soft. Your success will ultimately be determined by word of mouth. The association market is one of relationships, and the hard sell will quickly backfire. Remember that members expect that the services endorsed by the association are a cut above other services, and they will judge the services, not simply based on price and performance, but often on a company's sales and marketing techniques. If the member feels the company and sales force understands the members, the likelihood of sales increases.

NOTES

1. VISA U.S.A. "Affinity Cards Background Information" (August 1992), p. 1.
2. Andrew Barry, "Cracks in the Plastic", *Barrons* (November 18, 1991), p. 13.
3. "Mastercard Hopes to Close the Gap with Joint Ventures", *Washington Times* (September 13, 1992), p. A14.
4. "Affinity Cards Background Information", p. 1.
5. "Mastercard Hopes to Close the Gap with Joint Ventures", p. A14.
6. "Affinity Cards Background Information", p. 2.
7. "Are Retired People Different?" *Forbes* (September 14, 1992), p. 538.

Chapter Eight

Educational Opportunities

Partnership opportunities abound in the delivery of association group-purchasing programs, insurance, and financial services, but corporations often overlook the potential of associations for delivering educational programs and services. While associations are beginning to explore the world of broader member services, the main service of many associations remains education.

In fact, nearly 90 percent of associations, regardless of mission or membership, offer educational programs and services to their members and 71 percent disseminate public information.[1] It is estimated that association members spend $5.5 billion annually on association educational offerings. Of all the states in the nation, only the state of California spends more than associations to support higher education.[2] Many small businesses and professionals increasingly rely on their associations to provide the special skills critical for their business success, including management and employee training. In fact, associations now devote nearly $8.5 billion annually to adult education or specialized training.[3]

Several social and governmental factors contribute to the increasing role of associations as educators:

• The rapid pace of technological change. Members must keep pace with changes in the way they do business. While all members read about or are otherwise aware of new technologies, associations help their members answer these questions: How do new technologies affect the way I do businesses? Can the new ideas help me be more productive? What are my peers doing and how has it worked?

- Occupational specialization. For almost every discovery or new technology, new occupations and specialties are created. These specialties, in turn, generate educational needs often overlooked by the association that may represent the broader sector.
- America's restructuring. As American industry becomes leaner, industry is faced with the need to train existing staff for new positions and new skills. Laid-off employees are often faced with the need to retrain in order to be marketable. As America has deregulated, both businesses and professionals face new competitors with significantly different approaches. Associations provide a unique method by which traditional competitors can share information necessary to retain market share.
- Global competition. While most companies have faced competition from across the street, they now are facing increased pressure from around the world. Such competition requires companies to understand national customs, local business traditions, and even the impact of foreign currency fluctuations. Associations can supply this information efficiently and relate it directly to their memberships.
- Increased regulation. While government has deregulated the marketplace and increased competition, it has often increased the regulation imposed on individual businesses. The time spent by businesses and professionals to comply with new government regulations is staggering. The regulatory burden increases the need for employer knowledge of those regulations and employee education of those affected or saddled with their implementation. The challenge of new regulations is being able to interpret the regulation and determine how it will affect a business. Through peer education, associations are able to cut through the red tape and help members cope with new rules and challenges.
- More transient work force. Due in part to the restructuring of American business, the employee of today is less likely to be a career employee. No longer can the college graduate look to one employer to provide employment from graduation to retirement, for employers are less likely keep surplus

employees in hard times and employees are less likely to stand by a floundering employer. Through associations, businesses can provide a cost efficient method to train new employees in specific industry skills without the need to staff in-house training programs.

• Professionalism. Through the establishment of professional standards and related training programs, associations enable individuals to improve themselves and the image of their industry. As the public seeks greater assurance in the quality of their service providers and as businesses seek employees with known skills, association accreditation, certification, and licensing programs are growing rapidly.

• Public school shortfall. Unfortunately students have paid the price for the cutbacks in public school funding. Increasingly employers have found that graduates lack basic skills and are often functionally illiterate. It is estimated that 2.3 million illiterates are added to the U.S. work force every year, due to dropouts, immigration, and low-skilled high school graduates.[4] Therefore businesses must often teach the basics, such as reading and writing, before they are able to train in specific skills. A recent study by the American Management Association of 1,200 firms found that one-third of job seekers failed to score high enough on basic workplace tests to secure jobs. In response, it has been estimated that businesses now spend $25 billion annually on remedial education.[5]

EDUCATIONAL PROGRAMS

Association educational efforts are often narrowly thought of as group-study seminars, but as the needs and the audience for association programs have expanded, so have the methods used for their delivery. Generally associations offer both educational programs and services. Group study educational programs typically encompass seminars, conferences, conventions and teleconferences:

• Seminars. These are traditionally two- to three-day meetings dedicated to a particular topic. More recently, one-day seminars are increasingly popular, as businesses and professionals seek to reduce costs and keep the time away from their jobs to a minimum. It has been estimated that the average association conducts 11 educational seminars per year that attract an average 50 attendees and that, overall, association seminars attract over 20 million members annually.[6]

• Conferences. These meetings are designed to bring together conferees to share information and address various topics of concern, usually with multiple seminars or related interest sessions. Conferences are often utilized to highlight a sector of the association's activities or to offer a concentrated educational forum that addresses a broader topic area. It is also not unusual for conferences to include expositions that are relevant to the specific topic of the conference. One of the fastest-growing components of many conferences are peer-to-peer sessions, which permit members to gain from the experiences of other members. A recent conference of the American Society of Association Executive featured 225 peer sessions.

• Conventions/Trade Shows. Trade shows are big business for associations. In 1991, association conventions attracted almost 16 million delegates.[7] While many consider conventions as social events, conventions are increasingly focusing on education. It is not unusual for a convention to contain 10 or more hour to hour-and-a-half seminars, often referred to as "special interest sessions." In order to meet the expanding needs of their membership, many associations are now hosting multiple conventions and trade shows each year.

• Teleconferencing. With the advent of greater site availability and lower transmission costs, teleconferencing is becoming a viable alternative for educational delivery. While few associations depend on teleconferencing, it has proven to be a low-cost delivery system capable of reaching mass audiences.

While associations are significant providers of education, they often rely on partners to develop or deliver the programs and services. Since many associations have small staffs that often have a variety of responsibilities, associations look to outsiders to harness expertise, minimize start-up time, reduce risk, and provide additional marketing "legs".

• Expertise. Each company has an expertise in the products and services they offer. When packaged for associations and their memberships, such association-sponsored seminars enable the association to satisfy member needs while the company generates visibility, credibility, and a new revenue source. While associations are careful not to offer seminars that simply sell their partners' products and services, seminars do provide an excellent opportunity to introduce association members to a business and its representatives. The key to association seminar development is to make the association aware of your knowledge and willingness to assist the association. While some consultants and professionals, such as lawyers and accountants, have tapped the association market, corporations have largely ignored the potential. During 1990 and 1991, for example, 44 percent of associations that held seminars employed professional speakers or celebrities for the seminar.

• Reduce start-up time and risks. Often corporations have the ability to respond to educational needs quickly through the use of in-house training programs and marketing departments. These resources can be leveraged to address the needs of associations and their members. Often the very tools developed to train a company's sales force can be modified to educate its customers and prospects.

• Marketing legs. By harnessing the resources of a corporate partner with an association, the association often gains new marketing legs or advocates in the field. The association's partner usually has a sales force or marketing capability that can help generate interest in the seminar and in the association itself. The partnership enables the association to reach a broader audience and the corporate partner gains access to its targeted market.

Association educational partnerships usually involve the purchase of packaged programs or the development of seminars in conjunction with an expert or consultant. Generally, the effectiveness of packaged programs depends on the degree to which the programs can be customized to meet the needs of the association's membership. The more the vendor can relate the course to the association, the greater the chances of acceptance.[8]

The development of educational programs in conjunction with associations provides vendors with an established market and the association a method to stretch limited resources. Contracting out educational services frees up association time, taps new expertise and experience, and provides objectivity to the seminar or workshop. Associations will generally consider four criteria in the selection of educational instructors or contractors: credentials of the instructor, including academic and job experience, expertise in the area of instruction, quality of presentation, and the context of the proposed course in light of the instructor's expertise.[9]

EDUCATIONAL SERVICES

Association educational services include complimentary or alternative educational and informational distribution methods. While these services vary significantly between associations, the most common include the sale of books or pamphlets, video and audio cassettes, self-study programs, and computer-based learning services. Since most associations lack the in-house expertise and resources to develop such services, it is estimated that only 33 percent of associations now offer video training, 20 percent offer self-study programs and 7 percent offer computer-based learning, while a far larger percentage offer books and other publications for sale.[10]

Educational services are viewed as a critical member benefit by both associations and their members. A survey conducted of association members and nonmembers confirmed that members join associations to keep current about activities and issues, to establish professional contacts, to increase sales or professional credentials, and prefer to belong to an association that works to improve their industry or profession's image—all components of an association's educational and informational offerings.[11]

For producers and distributors of educational and informational products and services, associations are a hungry market for products that enable the association to satisfy a critical member need and the partner an effective alternative distribution channel.

ASSOCIATION PARTNERSHIP OPPORTUNITIES

Association educational partnerships range from association promotion to the coproduction of products and services. The ideal partnership will vary by association and the product being offered.

Association Promotion and Distribution

Associations represent an effective vehicle for the promotion of books, videos, and other products that are relevant to a particular industry or occupation. Since many associations review books in their publications or are receptive to prepared magazine articles relevant to their members, associations are an excellent way to target promotional efforts. Since most association magazines and newsletters accept advertising, educational products and services can be marketed directly to the association's members.

The bottom line is clear—by targeting your message through the association that represents your prospects, you eliminate wasted advertising and improve results.

Acropolis Books, a Washington, D.C.-area publisher, has found that associations represent an ideal, untapped resource for the promotion of books. "For every book, there is an association that represents potential readers who are interested in its topic or would benefit from its information," says John Hackl, a publishing consultant to associations. "An evaluation of the book's association promotion potential should be an integral part of a publisher's marketing process."

With more associations providing members with libraries of information specific to their industry, associations are rapidly becoming the research arms of members nationwide. When members seek advice on their business or profession, the resource recommendations of their association often generate sales for the products or publications. In 1991, the American Society of Association Executives replied to over 90,000 member inquiries, while the American Institute of Certified Public Accounts replied to over 64,000 member requests for information.[12]

Some associations are also willing to distribute educational products and services on behalf of its partners. Often the association offers its members a selection of educational products and services through a catalog provided to each member. The association usually reviews the materials and the members are able to purchase products relevant to their business or occupation. While the exact arrangements vary, the associations typically purchase the product at wholesale and then offer the products at retail or at a special member-discounted price. These association distribution partnerships enable the product or service to be offered to members with the support of the association, but not usually with its specific endorsement. If an association is receptive to providing distribution assistance, it may also be willing to support promotional efforts, such as the placement of articles which promote the product's usage or benefits or seminars which feature the publication's author or subject.

The American Trucking Associations (ATA) produces a catalog which provides member trucking companies with an array of educational and informational publications. While the catalog includes new regulations and association-developed materials, the association also distributes books and pamphlets produced by other publishers and companies of interest to the trucking industry.

Association Branding

Both association distribution and promotion can increase sales, but neither permits the product or service to carry the name or endorsement of the association. Branding offers the advantage of promoting the sale of books and other educational and information programs with the association's name, logo, and endorsement. Branding enables an existing product to be private-labeled for association marketing and promotion.

For example, many publishers now promote the sale of books by producing special association editions. These books usually feature forwards written by the association and carry the association's name or logo on the cover, back, or spine of the book. Through branding, publishers are able to provide works a new lease on life and boost sales. While many associations will distribute and promote branded books, others may also use the books as a premium or incentive to promote membership.

Acropolis Books has now produced three association editions of *100 Ways to Prosper in Today's Economy* by Barry R. Schimel. The special editions are customized for the supporting association by including information relevant to their memberships, enhancing the cover of the book, or permitting the association to provide a forward to the book. "Each new edition extends the

EXHIBIT 8–1
Two Special Editions of 100 Ways to Prosper in Today's Economy

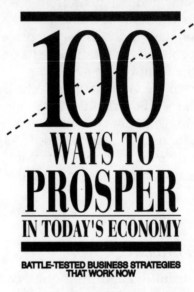

100
WAYS TO
PROSPER
IN TODAY'S ECONOMY

BATTLE-TESTED BUSINESS STRATEGIES
THAT WORK NOW

Barry R. Schimel, C.P.A.

Acropolis Books, Ltd.
Reprinted with permission of Acropolis Books Ltd.

book's market potential at minimum cost and risk to the association and the publisher," says John Hackl (see Exhibit 8–1).

Association Collaborations and Copublishing

While branding provides an effective means to promote published or established products, associations are often willing to collaborate in the publishing or production of new books or

EXHIBIT 8–1 (*Concluded*)

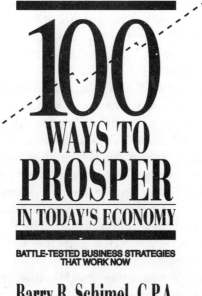

100

WAYS TO

PROSPER

IN TODAY'S ECONOMY

BATTLE-TESTED BUSINESS STRATEGIES
THAT WORK NOW

Barry R. Schimel, C.P.A.

Published for

AICPA
American Institute of Certified Public Accountants

by

Acropolis Books, Ltd.

educational services to meet member needs. In collaborations, the association is more actively involved in reviewing the manuscript or script, selecting trainers or authors, recommending sources, and supporting research efforts. While collaborative efforts are often limited to books, periodicals, and other educational and informational products, they are increasingly being utilized to deliver educational programs.

In order to provide its membership with relevant hands-on information, presented by experts at reasonable cost, the Healthcare Financial Management Association (HFMA) collaborates with corporations. HFMA represents 30,000 hospital chief financial officers who are responsible for administration, billing, and claims collection from government programs, third parties, and individuals. With 12 percent of the nations gross national product tied up in health care, the association's members exist where "money and sickness collide."

In collaboration with HFMA, Digital Equipment Corporation sponsors educational programs for association members which marry their knowledge of computers with applications relevant to hospital administration. Digital provides the faculty and works with the association to assure that the programs meet member needs. The HFMA also conducts for Digital Equipment a seminar entitled, "New to the Field," directed at their sales force and executives to provide them an overview of the health care finance field and the challenges faced by their members. The HFMA selects the faculty and develops the handouts for the Digital orientation seminars.

Al Sunseri, vice president of the Healthcare Financial Management Association, views the collaborations as win-wins. "Membership value is increased with improved speakers and programs at reduced cost due to the sponsorship, while the corporation gains valuable exposure and critical product development input." To ensure the integrity of the programs, Al Sunseri points out that "HFMA goes to great length to separate the sponsorship and the educational content—our members want education, not a sales pitch."

In collaborative efforts that involve the production of a publication or product, unlike promotional and distribution efforts, an association may also commit to buy or sell a minimum volume of the product, minimizing the partner's risk. While this collaborative process is more complicated, it can result in an association not only supporting marketing but viewing the product as part of an expanding and integral association menu. Rather than a distributor, the association becomes an advocate.

In copublishing, publishers or producers and the association share responsibility and risk in the product's production and sale. The association usually provides information or research that is central to the product, commits to the promotion and distribution of the product, and guarantees a minimum purchase for resale. The publisher or other partner provides technical support, is responsible for production, and distributes the final product through its usual channels. Copublishing is normally the preferred method for the production of materials that are industry- or occupational-specific and have unproven or small outside audiences.

While the American Institute of Certified Public Accountants (AICPA) publishes a significant number of publications annually, it also copublishes books with others. Copublishing enables the AICPA to market books that meet the needs of the membership while keeping development time to a minimum and harnessing the expertise available. With over 300,000 members nationwide, the AICPA, according to the director of publications, Robert P. Rainier, "seeks products that meet the needs of its members and the mission of the association, compete effectively with other products on the market, and, ideally, offer the ability for ongoing editions or updates."

It is important to note that associations also benefit from arrangements with commercial publishers by permitting the association to penetrate new or larger markets for the books it publishes. The association promotes the sale of the book to its membership and prospective members, while the commercial publisher distributes the books to other professionals and the public through bookstores nationwide. While most association publications will never reach the best-seller list, occasionally an association publication will become a commercial success.

The Naval Institute, an association of 110,000 regular reserve and retired officers of the Navy, Marine Corps, and Coast Guard, which is dedicated to the advancement of seapower, published its first work of fiction, a novel by Tom Clancy entitled *The Hunt for Red October*. While the Institute sold over 300,000 copies of the hardback edition, the paperback rights were sold to the commercial publisher Berkley/Jove Publishing Corporation of NewYork.[13] In addition, several other associations rely on commercial publishers for distribution of books and other products. While the Sierra Club booklist ranges from hiking guides, how-to-books, and a variety of fiction and nonfiction, the club's most recognized publications are its calendars, which sell in the millions each year.[14]

THE FUTURE

The delivery of information is becoming a technological challenge to many associations. As members demand more efficient and effective educational and information methods, the value of membership will be increasingly judged by the ability of the association to meet those needs. While associations have proved to be effective developers of mass educational programs such as seminars, conventions, and workshops, video and audio tapes, educational software, data bases, and CD-ROM, will require many associations to look to corporate partners to enable the association to continue to deliver critical education and information.

Marrying the expertise, resources, and marketing capability of a corporate partner with a targeted membership that relies on the association for information, education, and advice, can make a powerful combination indeed. When successful, the partnership will provide the membership with increased opportunities, the association with services that attract and retain members while generating non-dues income, and will provide the partner with increased visibility, credibility, and revenues.

EDUCATIONAL PROGRAMS AND SERVICES— KEYS TO SUCCESS

1. Know your prospects. Whether you produce training materials, books, videos, or other educational or informational services, determine which associations your current buyers or prospects belong to. By targeting your marketing through the associations that represent your buyers, marketing efficiency and sales can be increased.

2. Keep informed. Associations are more likely to be interested in programs and services that address current member needs or concerns. By keeping current with the challenges facing industries or professions, you can customize your program to meet the association's needs. Reading the association's magazine or newsletter is one way to keep up-to-date with the association and its members needs.

3. Become the association's expert. Make your company the one that the association turns to for advice. Lay the groundwork for educational programs and services by building the association's comfort and trust level. One option is to write articles for the association's magazine, a column for the association's newsletter, or advertise in these publications, addressing the question, "How does it (a new regulation, a recent trend, etc.) affect the membership and what actions should they take?"

Get to know the staff responsible for your area of expertise at the association and provide them an additional resource for information. Share with the association information that may affect their members, and, if you produce a client newsletter, add the association to the mailing list or press release mailings.

4. Road-test the idea. Take the time to discuss the project with the association to ensure that it meets the membership's and the association's goals. Countless hours can be saved by understanding the association's needs and its interest in the idea. Ask the association for input early on, and then keep them informed as you make progress. Don't forget to get the thoughts of some of your current customers, who may be association members— they can also provide excellent referrals.

5. Turnkey. Offer the association a solution to a problem, rather than more work. In your proposal identify the member problem or need, how your educational program or service will answer the need, what expertise and experience you have, and your implementation schedule.

6. Differentiate. Associations will often ask, "What does your service or program offer that the member can't receive elsewhere?" In educational programs, the answer will likely encompass the delivery of industry-specific expertise and advice, while in educational services you may provide increased access to specialized publications and preferred pricing.

7. Leverage your resources. You have the production expertise and resources and associations have critical marketing clout. All too often in educational services, companies view associations as competitors rather than potential partners. Associations have a constant need to meet their changing member needs and corporate partners enable them to respond quickly, avoid duplication, and reduce promotion, production, and distribution risks.

NOTES

1. American Society of Association Executives, *Associations Advance America* (ASAE, 1990) p. 6.

2. Ibid.

3. Ibid.

4. Daniel P. Oran, "Teacher Wanted. No Experience Necessary" *Business Week* (November 20, 1989), p. 82.

5. Fred Best and Ray Eberhard, "Education for the 'Era of the Adult' " *The Futurist* (May–June 1990), p. 23.

6. American Society of Association Executives, *Association Meeting Trends* (ASAE, 1992), p. xv.

7. Ibid.

8. American Society of Association Executives, *Association Education Handbook* (ASAE, 1984), p. 132.

9. Ibid., p. 129.

10. *Policies and Procedures in Association Management*, p. 95.

11. Foundation of the American Society of Association Executives, *The Decision to Join* (ASAE Foundation, 1981), p. 8.

12. Annual Reports of AICPA and ASAE.

13. Lys Ann Shore, "Quest for the Best Seller" *Association Management* (August 1986), p. 74.

14. Ibid.

Chapter Nine

A Prospecting Primer

Many corporations, with an association product idea in hand, launch head first into the association market, without any clear idea of their ideal association partner. Such untargeted efforts usually result in wasted effort and frustration and often harm corporate goodwill, as associations witness the corporation's poor preparation.

Association prospecting requires an analysis of associations that meet your needs, a review of your corporate sales and marketing, and a look in your own backyard.

THE ASSOCIATION PARTNER

Prospecting for the ideal association partner involves four steps:

1. Determining whether your target market is composed of businesses or individuals.
2. Determining whether your customers and prospects are located nationwide, statewide, or on a local basis.
3. Identifying whether your specific target market is a broad-based or a specialized market.
4. Determining what support is needed of your association partner.

Each of these steps will target your association prospecting by eliminating unsuitable associations and identifying those that meet your specific needs. These factors comprise the association prospecting matrix (Exhibit 9–1).

Step 1—Individuals or Businesses

There are two major types of associations: trade associations which represent businesses, and professional associations which represent individual members. If the target market for your

EXHIBIT 9–1
Association Prospecting Matrix

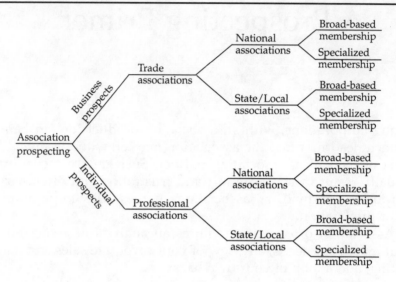

product or service is businesses, then a trade association is your natural candidate. On the other hand, if your target is individuals, then professional associations, which represent people with common occupations, vocations, or beliefs, may be ideal.

Remember that in some instances you may be able to approach the association market from both the trade and professional association viewpoint. For while your product or service may be used in business, the purchasing decision is likely to be made by an individual who may also be represented by another association.

Determining who your target market is has whittled your prospecting list in half—now you can concentrate on associations that represent your targeted businesses or individuals.

If, for example, your target is the banking and financial industry, over 400 national professional and trade associations represent this industry:*

---

*Source: *National Trade and Professional Associations of the U.S.* © 1993. Used with permission.

Trade associations	Professional associations
American Bankers Association	American Association of Bank Directors
American Finance Association	American Bankruptcy Institute
American Safe Deposit Association	National Association of Bank Loan and Credit Officers
Bank Administration Institute	Financial Women International
Independent Bankers Association of America	Association of Bank Holding Companies

Step 2—Where Are Your Customers or Prospects?

It is estimated that approximately one-third of all associations are national in scope, while two-thirds are state or local associations that represent businesses or individuals within a limited area and may be related to national associations. The ideal association is one that can compliment your existing sales and marketing efforts to increase your market share or one that can assist you in penetrating a new market or region.

If the products and programs you will be marketing are now available nationwide, a national association will usually be a natural fit. However a state or local association may provide a vehicle to test-market an association program that will be marketed outside of your normal sales and marketing channels.

If your program or services are now being marketed in only a few states or within a region, seeking the endorsement of a state or local association may enable you to increase your market share and leverage your local reputation. If you are seeking to expand your marketing outside of a limited market, a national association will be reluctant unless you have a clear marketing plan and resources to follow through. No association wants to launch a program that is unable to deliver. However, such a market expansion may be possible by seeking the endorsement of an adjoining state or local association and using the association's support as your marketing entry.

Step 3—Broad-Based or Specialized

Many associations represent a single industry or occupation. For example, there are over 400 national associations that represent banking and finance, 500 that represent education, and over 1,100 for science.[1] While some of these associations represent the broad-based industries or occupations, most represent sectors within an industry or specialists within an occupation. By determining the association that best represents your prospects, you can target both your association prospecting and, ultimately, your program marketing.

If, for example, your target is the legal profession, the American Bar Association represents 375,000 of America's practicing attorneys; however, 250 other national associations represent specialties and sectors of the legal community:*

American Foreign Law Association	Association of Legal Administrators
Association of Trial Lawyers	Christian Legal Society
Computer Law Association	Federal Bar Association
Hispanic National Bar Association	National Association of Black Women Attorneys
National Association of Women Lawyers	National Lawyers Guild
National Health Lawyers Association	Sports Lawyers Association

The exercise may seem daunting at first, but it will save time and often act as a catalyst for new ideas. The exercise will also provide an opportunity to rank associations, based on the marketing fit, from those who are ideal candidates to those that represent secondary alternatives.

Step 4—Association Support

At this point you have determined whether your target market is individuals or businesses and therefore whether the ideal association is a trade or professional association. You have also reviewed the merits of pursuing a national association versus a state or local association, based on the location of your prospects and customers. While the first two steps have reduced your prospecting list, you still need to examine what support you are seeking.

---

*Source: *National Trade and Professional Associations of the U.S.* © 1993. Used with permission.

When examining an association, first determine whether the association has the marketing vehicles to support your efforts, such as a magazine, newsletter, convention, and member data base, then consider the budget size. Remember that in most programs you are seeking a partner capable of supporting your marketing, not an association that will do your marketing. Therefore you are seeking first an association with the capability and credibility to communicate with its members.

The structure of an association can be critical if you are seeking a partner capable of performing specific marketing and sales functions. While most associations will not take orders, fulfill, bill, or drop ship products, some associations have formed service corporations which enable the association to take a more active marketing role.

The level of available support is often not easily determined; often interviewing the association provides the only clear picture of an association's capability and interest (see Chapter 10).

CORPORATE CONSIDERATIONS

While much of our discussion focuses on locating the ideal association, it is easy to forget that association programs have to be built on a company's existing foundation. Association partnerships represent a new method to target market; therefore it is important to consider the impact they may have on a corporation's existing sales and marketing structure. Often such considerations are ignored, and an association program, rather than being a catalyst for sales, becomes a management nightmare.

How Are Your Products or Services Sold?

Whether your products are sold via direct mail, company sales force, or independent sales representatives, the impact of an association program can't be overlooked. If your current sales efforts depend on direct mail, associations may provide an excellent vehicle to target the message and increase overall response rates. Be prepared to customize your mailings to reflect the association's name and logo in order to appeal to the

members' affinity and loyalty. Take time to examine your response rates and segregate those individuals or businesses who
have exhibited high response rates. Often, by interviewing these
high response buyers you may be able to determine which associations they belong to and short-cut your prospecting.

If your current sales efforts rely on a corporate sales force, you
may be able to motivate your sales people by providing them
with quality sales leads of motivated association members. The
key is to involve your sales force in the association prospecting
process, for your sales force can be your eyes and ears, able to
interview customers to determine their association loyalties.

If you depend on third-party organizations to market your
products, associations may represent a challenge. One of the keys
to association programs is to ensure the member's confidence in
the program's quality and pricing. Often, independent sales
forces market the products or services of other companies; therefore, companies should be prepared to answer, "How can the association be assured that its endorsement is being used only to
market the intended products or services?"

Can You Maintain Pricing Integrity?

Many corporations permit regional or local offices to set prices
based on competition. While such pricing flexibility may be desirable, it can be a nightmare in association programs where the
parties agree to offer products at a discounted fixed price or a
percentage off of the list price. After all, what value does the
member receive when the price the association offers is higher
than the price he may have been able to negotiate on his own?

Some strategies which may enable an association program to
co-exist with regional or local pricing include:

• Restricting the products offered through the association to
new products. This approach will eliminate conflicts with existing products and their pricing approaches.

• Examining the most commonly offered local discounts and
negotiating an association price that ensures competitiveness.
By surveying the pricing offered through regional offices to
the membership of the association, you can ensure that the

pricing offered is indeed better than that available to members purchasing on an individual basis.

• Offering a discount or rebate on the best price available. This approach can ensure that all members receive an advantage from the association program but may make advertising the program difficult and generate dissatisfaction among some members who are unable to negotiate pricing as low as other members. In light of the proliferation of automobile rebating, some members may conclude that the rebate has simply been added to the price and doubt the offering's value.

• Providing products that have been customized to meet the association's specification or needs—essentially establishing a new product. This approach ensures that members are purchasing a product or program that is not easily available elsewhere and has been modified to meet the members' specific needs.

• Offering preferred financing, leasing, warranties, or service contracts that differentiate the program or products from those currently available to the association's members. Often members judge an offering not simply based on price but on the ease of purchase and the assurance of ongoing support.

What Is Your Marketing Philosophy?

Associations are relationship-driven organizations. Association partnerships will often succeed or fail, not because of product performance, but because of inadequate or inappropriate sales and marketing efforts. Association partnerships are not a marketing panacea, but a highly effective target-marketing alternative that relies on the ongoing commitment of its corporate partner.

Corporations that are seeking instant results or believe that the simple endorsement of an association will replace existing sales and marketing efforts will be disappointed. On the other hand, companies that are committed to serving their targeted market, providing top quality service, and, as a result, generating increased sales and market share, will not be disappointed.

Does Your Company or Product Face Any Licensing Hurdles That Would Impact Its Marketing?

Some products, such as insurance and other financial products, are heavily regulated at the state level and the ability to expand to meet the needs of a national association's membership may not be easy or quick. Choose associations that represent members in states where you are currently in the process of obtaining the required licensing. There is nothing more frustrating to an association than members that can't participate in an association program.

Does Your Company Understand the Competitive Environment in Markets Outside of Its Existing Territory?

While some programs may be very competitive in a local market, they may face different competitive challenges in other areas of the country. Select associations that represent members in areas where your program is most competitive. This approach ensures that your marketing pays off and that members receive real value.

YOUR OWN BACKYARD

Your best association candidates may be in your own backyard. Take the time to examine those associations that already know you and the quality of your products and services:

Which Associations Do Your Customers Belong to?

Your best customers can provide a powerful door-opener to their association. Your sales force is well-positioned to make inquiries, and if your company markets more than one product or service, the customers of each product or service will belong to one or more professional or trade associations at the national and state level. By working with those associations that represent your most active buyers and prospects, you can build on your track record.

Which Associations Do You Support?

Many companies find that they are already supporting associations which represent their prospects through trade shows, exhibitions, convention attendance, and advertising in the association's magazine or newsletter. In addition, while most associations prohibit suppliers from joining an association as voting members, most do have associate or supplier memberships.

These memberships usually provide some limited marketing access, such as exhibit space rental, convention registration, and magazine advertising.

Your proven support of the association can provide a powerful door-opener to your ideal association. You have invested in establishing goodwill—why not take advantage of it?

PROSPECTING SUMMARY

By completing the prospecting matrix, reviewing your company sales and marketing structure and exploring your own backyard, you have identified key association attributes and identified a few association prospects.

Program Prospects	*Association Targets*
Individual purchasers	Professional associations
Business purchasers	Trade associations
Nationwide prospects	National associations
State/local prospects	State and local associations
Broad industry appeal	Broad-based associations
Specific sector interest	Specialty associations

THE BOTTOM LINE

Know your product and your prospects before you begin to identify association partners. With some homework, you can ensure that the association represents your targeted market, matches your marketing capability, and is able to compliment your sales efforts—the ingredients to a successful program.

A PROSPECTING PRIMER WORKSHEET

The Association Partner

1. Are your prospects businesses or individuals? Businesses are represented by trade associations, while individuals and

professionals are represented by professional societies or individual membership organizations.

Remember, that while the ultimate purchaser may be a business, the buying decision may be made by an individual who can be reached through a professional society.

Be specific as you examine and define your prospects; the more specific, the greater chances of success. If you sell to doctors, for example, do they work in individual practices, clinics or hospitals? What specialty do they practice? Who are their patients? Each answer pinpoints additional association avenues.

2. Where are your customers? Are they generally concentrated in a geographic area, perhaps due to geographic nature of your product or your sales force and distribution capabilities? Associations are generally more interested in programs that are capable of reaching a majority of their membership. National associations are rarely interested in programs that are capable of supporting members in only six states.

Remember, although you may be marketing in a limited area, most associations only represent members in a limited area. By locating associations that overlap your marketing map, you will frequently also find associations that are familiar with your product and your reputation. A good regional association success story makes a great stepping stone to its national association parent.

3. Can your prospects best be reached through a broadly based membership association or one that represents a sector of the business or profession? Associations offer the ability to target audiences within targets. After all, why prospect to 100,000 members who happen to share a common profession, when only 10,000 actually practice the specialty that uses your product?

The more targeted your prospecting becomes, the more relevant your program becomes to the association's membership and the more interested the association will be.

4. What association marketing support is needed? Determine what communication channels the association has available to reach its members and assist you in marketing your program. If

you have an active sales force, marketing campaign, and advertising program, the association should be able to support your efforts and enhance your credibility.

Corporate Considerations

1. How are your products sold? The ideal association should mesh with your ability to support sales and program support to its members. While direct mail has few boundaries, companies that support sales need to ensure that they can control the quality and pricing that is offered through the association.

While company sales forces usually present little difficulty, companies that utilize third-party marketing are often unable to ensure consistent quality and product availability.

2. Can you maintain price integrity? Most association programs offer a discount off list price or a lower set price; therefore companies need to be able to ensure that members receive the agreed-upon terms. Often companies, for example, permit regional pricing flexibility to meet the competition. While this flexibility will enable some members to receive better prices, other members may receive less attractive pricing, or, worse, the regularly offered local price may be better than the association-negotiated price.

Associations want to be assured that the program offered provides real value to members. Often, by restricting the association program to specific or new products, the problem can be minimized.

3. What is your marketing philosophy? Association business is a relationship business and therefore a long-term investment. While the association's name and goodwill will open doors, the long-term success is still in the hands of the corporate partner. If you are looking for a short-term fix, skip the association market.

Your Backyard

1. Which associations do your customers belong to? Why not do business with the association that represents your best

customers? If they are happy, others will be. Your sales force is your eyes and ears; use them to ferret out prospective associations.

2. Which association do you support? The associations at which you exhibit, attend conventions, advertise in their magazines, or those to whom you belong as a corporate member, likely represent your prospects and are aware of your support.

Don't overlook your sales force; often your sales people have joined local associations within their territories, and these can make excellent starting points.

Chapter Ten

Targeting the Association

At this point you have likely determined, based on the prospecting matrix, whether your ideal association is a professional or trade association, national or local association, and represents a broad-based or specialized membership. Perhaps you have also identified, through interviews with customers and by examining your backyard, a few potential association suitors. In any case, the process of targeting your association has just begun.

The key to successful association prospecting is to know the association: its membership, budget, staff, and its desire to attract members and build nondues income. Some of the information is easily available, but homework will be required to fully develop the prospecting picture. A recent survey of association executives found that a vendor's sales success depends largely on the relevancy of the message to the association's needs, yet most suppliers simply don't take the time to understand the association and its needs and subsequently waste the opportunity.[1]

Many tools of the trade are available which can expedite your work; with the help of directories, data bases, direct-mail lists, and associations themselves, you can narrow the field and target only those associations that meet your needs.

DIRECTORIES

Association directories fall into two categories: those that provide data on the association and those that provide information on the association's personnel. For the purposes of prospecting for associations, an organizational directory will be more useful, although the personnel directory can serve as a further reference once particular associations have been identified.

While association organization directories differ in their exact contents and association profile information, most contain:

Association's name

Telephone and fax numbers

Organization's purpose

Membership size

Staff size

Address

Executive name and title

Historical background

Annual budget

Publications and conventions

Often the most important consideration is not the data itself but how the directory is indexed. After all, most of the time you will not be looking up a specific association but seeking information regarding associations that serve a particular industry or occupation. While most directories index alphabetically by association name, others also index by industry, occupation, budget, location, and even association acronyms. Each index saves time and eliminates wasted prospecting efforts. It is easy to assume, for example, that an association called the ABA is the American Bar Association, but in fact 16 national associations have ABA as their acronym—ranging from the 375,000-member American Bar Association to the 1,000-member American Bison Association.

Sample listings from two leading national association directory publishers are shown in Exhibits 10–1 and 10–2.

It is important to note that many other directories are available that provide information on regional, local, and international associations. These directories provide information similar to that of national association directories and often include information on the relationship of the state, local, or international association to other associations (see Exhibits 10–3, 10–4, and 10–5).

While many directories concentrate on the association's organization, personnel directories also provide the prospector specific staffer names within the association. These directories tend to be published by associations that represent associations

EXHIBIT 10–1

Sample National Association Listing

American Soc. of Ass'n Executives (1920)
1575 Eye St., N.W., Washington DC 20005-1168
Tel: (202) 626-2723   *Fax:* (202) 371-8825
President: R. William Taylor, CAE
Members: 20,000 individuals   *Staff:* 125
Annual Budget: over $5,000,000
Hist. Note: Founded in Lenox, Massachusetts in 1920 as
American Trade Ass'n Executives, a successor organization to
the Nat'l Trade Organization Secretaries. Name changed in
1956 to American Soc. of Ass'n Executives. A professional
society of paid employees of associations and societies.
Certifies association executives and awards the CAE (Certified
Association Executive) designation. Sponsors the ASAE
Foundation and A-PAC. Has an annual budget of
approximately $15 million. Membership: $155/year.
Publications:
     Association Management. m. adv.
     Who's Who in Association Management. a. adv.
     Leadership Magazine. a.
     International News. bi-m. adv.
     Association Law & Policy. bi-w.
     Government Relations. bi-m.
     Dollars & Cents. m.
     Association Educator. bi-m.
     Meetings and Expositions. m.
     Membership Marketer. m.
     Associate Member Update. q.
     Communication News. m.
Tri-annual Meetings: March/2,000, August/4,000 and
     December/2,000
     1993-Orlando, FL/March 27-31
     1993-Minneapolis, MN/Aug. 21-25
     1993-Chicago, IL/Dec. 12-15
     1994-Washington, DC/March 5-9
     1994-San Francisco, CA/Aug. 27-31
     1994-Washington, DC/Dec. 11-14
     1995-Indianapolis, IN/March 11-15
     1995-Washington, DC/Aug. 12-16
     1995-Chicago, IL/Dec. 11-14
     1996-Washington, DC/March 9-13
     1996-Chicago, IL/July 20-24

Reprinted with permission of the *National Trade and Professional Associations of the U.S.*
© 1993.

themselves, such as the American Society of Association Executives and many of its allied societies. These directories often list members alphabetically and by association (see Exhibit 10–6).

ELECTRONIC ACCESS

Another prospecting option is to access association information electronically through data bases or CD-ROM. This option permits the user to search for associations based on selected fields of information, such as the association's name, association acronym, keyword in the association's name, city or state, number of members, budget size, or descriptive text. The *Encyclopedia of*

EXHIBIT 10–2
Sample National Association Listing

★12369★   AMERICAN DENTAL HYGIENISTS' ASSOCIATION (Dentistry)
(ADHA)
444 N. Michigan Ave., Ste. 3400   Phone: (312)440-8929
Chicago, IL 60611   Kathleen Bell, Exec.Dir.
Founded: 1923. Members: 30,000. Staff: 39. Budget: $4,200,000.
Regional Groups: 12. State Groups: 53. Local Groups: 360. Professional
organization of licensed dental hygienists possessing a degree or certificate in
dental hygiene granted by an accredited school of dental hygiene. Administers
Dental Hygiene Candidate Aptitude Testing Program and makes available
scholarships, research grants, and continuing education programs. Maintains
accrediting service through the American Dental Association's (see separate
entry) Commission on Dental Accreditation. Bestows awards; compiles
statistics. Computerized Services: Data base; mailing list services. Telecommunications Services: Fax, (312)440-8929; toll-free number,
(800)243-ADHA. Committees: Education; Member Services; National
Boards; Public Relations; Regulation and Practice; Research; Scholarship.
Divisions: Communications; Government Affairs; Member Services; Professional Development.

Publications: *American Dental Hygienists' Association Access*, 10/year.
Magazine covering current dental hygiene topics, regulatory and legislative
developments, and association news. Includes membership profiles and
course offerings. Price: Included in membership dues; $18/year for
nonmembers. Circulation: 30,000. Advertising: accepted. ● *Dental Hygiene*, 9/year. Professional journal; includes association news, book reviews,
abstracts, government news, and information on research and new products.
Price: Included in membership dues; $40/year for nonmembers. ISSN:
0091-3979. Circulation: 30,000. Advertising: accepted. Alternate Formats: microform.

Convention/Meeting: annual (with exhibits) - 1993 June 9-16, Dever, CO.

From *Encyclopedia of Associations*, 27th ed. Vol. 1–3, Part 1–3, ed. Deborah M. Burek.
Gale Research, Inc. © 1993. Reproduced by permission of the publisher.

Associations, published by Gale Research, is available through
both DIALOG data base and CD-ROM GlobalAccess: Associations.

The *Encyclopedia of Associations* data base contains information
on over 90,000 nonprofit membership organizations, including
national, regional, state, local, and international associations—
the equivalent of 13 volumes of printed data. The information is
gathered by annual questionnaires mailed to association executives, and 4,500 new listings are added annually (see Exhibits
10–7 and 10–8).

As with any target marketing, associations are of course available for direct-mail campaigns. The "bible" of direct mail lists is

EXHIBIT 10–3
Sample State/Local Association Listing

New York Soc. of Ass'n Executives (1919)
322 8th Ave., 12th Floor, New York NY 10001-8001
Tel: (212) 206-8230   *Fax:* (212) 645-1147
President: Joel A. Dolci, CAE
Members: 950   *Staff:* 8
Annual Budget: $500-1,000,000
Hist. Note: An allied society of the American Soc. of Ass'n
Executives (Washington, DC), NYSAE represents the
educational and professional needs of regular and associate
members from non-profit organizations and supplier firms in
the metroplitan New York area. Regular members are
association staff members managing trade, professional,
technical, educational or philanthropic associations. Associate
members offer products and services to the association
community. Membership: $125/year (regular); $245/year
(associate).
Publications:
Association Executive 7/year. adv.
Membership Directory. a. adv.
Educational Planning Guide. a. adv.
Association Profile Book. a.
Data and Word Processing Survey. a.
Salary Survey. a.
Annual Meetings: February, in New York City/1,500

Reprinted with the permission of *State and Regional Associations of the U.S.* © 1993.

EXHIBIT 10–4
Sample State/Local Association Listing

★3678★   GREAT LAKES LIGHTHOUSE KEEPERS ASSOCIATION
(GLLKA)
PO Box 580   Phone: (313)426-4150
Allen Park, MI 48101   Richard L. Moehl, Pres.
Founded: 1982. **Members:** 1100. Individuals interested in the
historical preservation and restoration of lighthouses on the Great Lakes;
those seeking contact with the descendants of lighthouse keepers on the
Great Lakes. Acts as a clearinghouse of information concerning
restoration projects; seeks to develop a listing of groups that have
completed or are in any phase of a restoration project. Compiles
statistics; conducts research programs. **Formerly:** (1983) Lighthouse
Keepers Association.

Publications: *The Beacon,* quarterly. Newsletter. ● *Index to the GLLKA
Oral History Tape Collection,* periodic.

Convention/Meeting: annual conference.

From *Encyclopedia of Associations: Regional, State and Local Organizations,* Third ed., vol.
1–4, ed. by Grant J. Eldridge. Gale Research, Inc. © 1993. Reproduced by permission
of the publisher.

EXHIBIT 10–5
Sample International Association Listing

★5007★   ASSOCIATION **MONTESSORI** INTERNATIONALE (AMI)
Koninginneweg 161   Phone: 20 6798932
NL-1075 CN Amsterdam, Netherlands   G.J. Portielje, Pres.
Founded: 1929. **Members:** 3000. **Staff:** 2. **National Groups:** 30.
Languages: English. **Multinational.** Individuals, Montessori societies or institutions, subscribers, teacher training centers, and others interested in furthering the ideas and principles of Dr. Maria Montessori (1870-1952), Italian physician and educator. (The Montessori method, as developed by Montessori, stresses the development of the child's initiative and sense of muscle training by using specially prepared teaching materials and games; it also emphasizes the freedom of the child with the teacher as a supervisor and guide rather than as formal instructor.) Aims are to: propagate the Montessori method, spreading knowledge of the physical, intellectual, moral, social, and mental development of the child, from conception to maturity, at home and in society; demonstrate the importance of the child in and for the progress of civilization; promote recognition of the child's fundamental rights as envisaged by Montessori, irrespective of racial, religious, political, or social environment; cooperate with other bodies and organizations that promote the development of education, human rights, and peace. Accredits centers to prepare adults to work with normal, handicapped, and emotionally disturbed children, in various age groups. Advises on the manufacture of Montessori material; provides for the publication of Montessori's book in different languages; initiates and guides other activities such as the Help the Children Project in developing countries. Conducts study conferences, seminars, and lectures. **Telecommunications Services:** Fax, 20 6767341. **Committees:** Executive; Material; Pedagogical; Sponsoring.

Publications: *Communications*, quarterly. Magazine.

Convention/Meeting: periodic congress.

From *Encyclopedia of Associations: International Organizations*, 27th ed., Part 1 & 2, ed. by Linda Irvin. Gale Research, Inc. © 1993. Reproduced by permission of the publisher.

EXHIBIT 10–6
Sample Association Executive Listing

Taylor, R. William, CAE, Pres
Amer Soc of
Assn Execs
1575 Eye St NW
Washington, DC 20005-1168
202/626-2723RG

From *Who's Who in Association Management*, the American Society of Association Management. © 1993. Reproduced with permission.

EXHIBIT 10–7
DIALOG: National Association Listing

1/9/1
09996544 EA ENTRY NO.: 003457 (National Organizations of the U.S.)
National Federation of Independent Business (NFIB)
150 W. 20th Ave., San Mateo, CA 94403
(415) 341-7441
William Critzer, Exec.V.Pres.
FOUNDED: 1943. MEMBERS: 560,000. STAFF: 225. Field Staff: 675. BUDGET:
$52,000,000. Independent business and professional people. Presents
opinions of small and independent business to state and national
legislative bodies. Members vote by ballot on issues; ballots are tabulated
and results forwarded to legislators. Conducts surveys at the state level
with area directors and government affairs representatives working with
state legislatures. Maintains 50 person legislative, research, and public
affairs office in Washington, DC. Compiles statistics. COMMITTEES:
Political Action.
PUBLICATIONS: Independent Business, bimonthly. * NFIB Mandate, bimonthly.
* Also prepares and disseminates weekly press releases to daily papers,
trade associations, and chambers of commerce nationwide, and monthly
materials to high schools, colleges, and universities throughout the U.S.
CONVENTION/MEETING: quadrennial.
SECTION HEADING CODES: Trade, Business, and Commercial Organizations (01)
DESCRIPTORS: Small Business

From *Encyclopedia of Associations*, 27th ed. © 1993. Reproduced by permission of the
publisher.

EXHIBIT 10–8
DIALOG: Regional, State, and Local Listing

2/9/2
01996715 EA ENTRY NO.: 003288 (Regional, State and Local Organizations)
California Redwood Association (CRA)
405 Enfrente Dr., No. 200, Novato, CA 94949
(415) 382-0662
Christopher F. Grover, Exec.V.Pres.
FOUNDED: 1916. MEMBERS: 9. STAFF: 14. Represents manufacturers of redwood
lumber products. Serves as a source of technical information for all who
study, sell, or buy redwood products.
PUBLICATIONS: Pamphlets of technical information on lumber and building
and data files.
CONVENTION/MEETING: annual - always second Tuesday in September, Eureka,
CA.
SECTION HEADING CODES: WESTERN STATES (5)
DESCRIPTORS: Forest Industries

From *Encyclopedia of Associations*, Regional, State, and Local Organizations. © 1993.
Reproduced by permission of the publisher.

the Standard Rate and Data Service (SRDS), which is a comprehensive listing of sellers of direct-mail lists that covers almost any subject, including associations and their executives. SRDS is available in most larger public libraries (see Exhibit 10–9).

Most companies who publish directories also offer mailing lists, which are based on the directories' data and usually are generated by type of association, scope of the association (national, state, etc.), budget, staff, location, industry, and position titles. These mailing lists are ideal for companies seeking to market a product or program believed to be of mass appeal, rather than of specific interest to a narrower list of association prospects.

In addition, many associations that represent association executives rent their membership lists to interested companies. These mailing lists are very accurate since they are based on the membership roster of the association and are updated on a continual basis.

ASSOCIATION ASSISTANCE

Yes, even association executives have their own associations. Lead by the 20,000-member American Society of Association Executives, 69 domestic state or local allied societies, and 8 international societies, these associations provide their association executive members with education and information, encourage high ethical standards, and acquire and disseminate data on the functions and accomplishments in association management.

These associations of association executives also provide prospecting assistance for vendors seeking access to many of the key association leaders. Through associate membership, expositions, and an array of conferences, these associations provide an opportunity to learn more about associations and their marketing opportunities. The Chicago Society of Association Executives (CSAE), like many of its counterparts, provides businesses membership access, including trade show exhibition, publications, directories, sponsorship opportunities, associate membership, and membership list rental.

EXHIBIT 10–9
Direct Mail Listings

ASSOCIATIONS YELLOW BOOK-MONITOR PUBLISHING

Location ID: 13 ICLS 45   Mid 072431-000

1. PERSONNEL
List Manager
Affinity Marketing Group, Inc., 9663 C Main St., P.O. Box 2409, Fairfax, VA 22032. Phone 703-978-4927. FAX 703-978-7832.

2. DESCRIPTION
Recipients of a directory of the leading trade and professional associaitions in the U.S. providing information on officers, directors, managers, professional staff and top administrators.

4. QUANTITY AND RENTAL RATES
Rec'd Aug. 21, 1992.

	Total Number	Price per/M
Total list	38,244	85.00
Job function:		
Head person	1,094	+5.00
Officers/management	11,468	"
Washington representative	811	"
Political action representative	261	"
Committee member	1,938	"
Board member	22,313	"
Publisher	392	"
Branch	490	"

Selections: industry, state, SCF, ZIP Code, 5.00/M extra; key coding, 2.00/M extra; phone numbers, 15.00/M extra. Minimum order 250.00.

5. COMMISSION, CREDIT POLICY
Unlimited usage, double base rate.

6. METHOD OF ADDRESSING
4-up Cheshire labels. Pressure sensitive labels, 8.00/M extra. 3" x 5" cards, 10.00/M extra. Magnetic tape, 25.00 flat fee. Diskette, 25.00/M.

8. RESTRICTIONS
Sample mailing piece required for approval.

11. MAINTENANCE
Update semiannually.

AMERICAN LIST COUNSEL'S ASSOCIATIONS

Location ID: 10 DCLS 548   Mid 024304-008
Member: D.M.A.
American List Counsel, Inc.
88 Orchard Rd., CN-5219, Princeton, NJ 08543. Phone 201-874-4300, Toll free, 800-526-3973, FAX, 201-874-4433.
NOTE: For basic information on the following numbered listing segments 1, 5, 6, 7, 9, 10, 11, see American List Counsel, Inc. listing in Established Domestic Business Lists section under classification No. 46.

2. DESCRIPTION
National headquarters of American associations. ZIP Coded in numerical sequence 100%. List is computerized.

3. LIST SOURCE
Directories.

4. QUANTITY AND RENTAL RATES
Rec'd March 3, 1992.

	Total Number	Price per/M
National headquarters	19,916	50.00
Directors by name	19,553	55.00
Agricultural	983	"
Athletic & sport	751	"
Cultural	1,638	"
Educational	1,203	"
Fraternal/foreign interest	509	"
Government public admn./military	684	"
Greek letter	321	"
Health & medical	1,939	"
Hobby	1,353	"
Labor unions/assn./fed.	223	"
Public affairs	1,833	"
Religious	1,100	"
Science/engineering/technical	1,278	"
Social welfare	1,538	"
Trade/business/commerce	3,600	"
Veterans	444	"

Selections: state, 3.00/M extra; title addressing, 2.50/M extra; SCF, ZIP Code, number of members, 5.00/M extra; key coding, 1.00/M extra; phone numbers 10.00/M extra. Minimum order 150.00 plus selections.

From *Direct Mail Rates & Data*, October, 1992, published by Standard Rate and Data. Used with permission.

According to CSAE's executive director, Chris Mahaffey, "Membership in societies of association executives provides corporations the ability to build relationships and establish common bonds with fellow members and business associates. By investing in the relationship, corporations get to know both the business and the needs of associations."

It is important to note that while most of ASAE's allied societies represent state or local associations, some, especially those located in Washington, D.C. (the Greater Washington Society of Association Executives), New York (New York Society of Association Executives), and Chicago (Chicago Society of Association Executives) are composed primarily of national or international associations headquartered in their metropolitan areas.

These societies also provide association executives a forum to exchange ideas and discuss problems common to their organizations. Since two of the key concerns of associations are membership and nondues income, association executives rely on their association magazines to keep them current on services, trends and companies interested in working with associations.

One of the most effective broadcast prospecting tools is to advertise in the magazines that association executives read, such as *Association Management*, the magazine of the American Society of Association Executives, and similar publications of the allied societies. These association magazines are targeted at their respective association executive members and enable the vendor to target a message specifically to the association market. The advertisements can compliment sales and marketing efforts and reinforce your corporate interest and commitment to associations and the members they serve.

Association Management, for example, provides advertisers with complementary marketing opportunities, including three national trade shows, the opportunity to rent its mailing list of association members, and advertising campaign assistance.

The magazines of association executives also provide an excellent way to keep your marketing and sales forces aware of issues relevant to association executives and events, such as conventions and trade shows, that may be available to reach the association market.

ADDITIONAL RESEARCH

It is tempting, with a list of association candidates in hand, to lick the stamps and send the letters—but most of the effort will be wasted and much of the mail will go unopened. Association executives report receiving over 200 letters a week, most of which have no relevance to the association's needs. Simply knowing that the association exists, its address, staff size, and budget doesn't answer the bottom line question—are they interested and motivated?

With a short list of prospective associations, seek out additional information regarding the association, its communication vehicles, its attitude toward member services, and its need for nondues income.

• Call the association and request information. Many associations publish information for membership recruitment that provides insight into the organization, its mission, programs, and services.

• Inquire as a potential advertiser. Since most larger associations publish magazines or newsletters and over 50 percent accept advertising, most produce a media kit. Usually these kits include a sample magazine or newspaper and, more importantly, demographic data on their members and their buying habits.

• Inquire as a potential corporate member. Most associations permit suppliers to join as associates or corporate members. Such membership information normally contains an overview of the association, its publications, trade shows, and conventions.

• Ask a member. It is likely that some of your best customers are members of your target association. Ask your customers to secure association information for your review and interview your customers regarding their attitudes toward the association and its services.

With the assistance of directories, electronic access, direct-mail lists, association magazines, and association inquiries, you have now assembled a list of associations that may meet your key litmus tests. Two options are available: direct mail interested or targeted associations, or call the association—both with one goal—to interview association candidates.

THE DIRECT MAIL OPTION

Deciding which individuals to contact is one of the most critical decisions in direct mailing. Most association directories contain the name of the association's CEO, usually titled executive director, executive vice president, or president. While these executives can be directly targeted in smaller associations, in larger associations the bureaucracy is similar to that in many large corporations, and more research may enable you to locate the staff responsible for services development. For these associations, often the easiest method is to call the association and ask to talk with the individual in charge of services, usually called director of services, services manager, or member services manager.

Direct mail enables you to broadcast your interest to many associations at one time at low cost. The challenge is getting the attention of association executives who are facing the same mail glut as you. It is amazing how much of the mail associations receive is obviously untargeted and therefore unrelated to the association or its members. Such mail has little chance of being read, and, worse, if read reflects poorly on the corporate suitor.

A survey of association executives found that a well-designed direct-mail packet should include three components: a cover letter, a product or service description, and several response options.

Cover Letter

The purpose of the cover letter is to get the attention of the association executive, introduce your program and its benefits, build confidence, and generate response. The ideal association letter should accomplish these goals in one page. The first three lines of a well-designed cover letter should grab the association's attention and demand its further reading. The lines should ideally refer to the members of the particular association rather than simply "association members"; the more customized the letter, the more likely is the association to respond. Personalizing the first three lines might also include using a quote from an association member, using survey facts, or including a quote from the association's magazine or newsletter.

The next two or three paragraphs should detail the benefits of providing such a program and how the program will help the association satisfy a membership need. Don't attempt to provide a detailed description of the program or proposal; your objective here is to interest the association, not to present a packaged program.

Your goal is to build the confidence of the association in your ability and experience. Be specific—discuss your experience in serving the association's members and understanding their needs. Exhibit your ability by providing a corporate snapshot and your commitment to the programs successful implementation and marketing support. Stress the turnkey nature of your program and your ability to customize it for the association's specific needs.

The easier it is for an executive to reply, the greater the response rate. Most association executives favor the use of a postage paid reply card or, at a minimum, a toll-free telephone number. Consider the use of a premium, but keep it related to the product, such as an industry report or survey regarding the product's usage or growing acceptance.

One of the most effective ways of reinforcing a key point, one that almost always gets read, is adding postscripts (PS or even PPS) to your letters. Don't waste the opportunity to remind your reader of the program's most important benefit to the members or the association.

Product Pamphlet

Illustrations and simplicity are the keys to a successful product pamphlet. Keep the text to a minimum and let the products talk for themselves. If your proposal offers a line of products to the association, be sure that the products illustrated are appropriate to the association and its members. If, for example, you are attempting to sell copiers to an association that represents small businesses, your pamphlet should not highlight high-volume, big-ticket copiers.

An alternative to using a product pamphlet might be to include an example of your marketing capability, such as a customer newsletter or simply a list of references, preferably of association members who are clients or of other associations that you work with.

Response Options

Don't make the association have to look for a way to respond; include your toll-free phone number and fax number on all pieces of the mailing, since many times the executive who receives your package will refer various pieces to others for review. In addition, including a postage-paid reply card can provide an easy method for associations to reply.

Many companies have had great success including a survey as an additional response option. The survey usually includes questions to gauge the association's attitudes toward services, its membership, and the needs of the membership regarding the product or service being offered, and to solicit information regarding the association's organization and key personnel. Ideally the survey should be kept to one page in length, and you should include a self-addressed prepaid reply envelope and fax number to encourage response.

The response rate to surveys can often be increased by offering the association an executive summary of the responses. This adds credibility to the survey and gives the association an incentive to provide the information, since association executives are often interested in the attitudes and services being offered by other associations.

THE INTERVIEW

Whether or not you have employed direct mail or simply have identified associations that meet your needs, interviewing the association offers a unique opportunity to evaluate the suitability of your prospect and judge whether the association can meet your expectations and sales goals. The right association and the right product can bring both parties their desired goals. The vendor gains an active advocate and a targeted receptive market, while the association gains nondues income and the ability to acquire and retain members through offering a valuable service.

Perhaps the most important element of the interview is to remember who requested it and for what purpose. Surprisingly, many companies request interviews and then waste the opportunity once it's granted. The interview is *your* interview of the association and should be conducted to gain the knowledge necessary to determine whether program development is merited. While your research has pinpointed associations that meet your basic parameters, interviews enable you to determine your ideal partner. Unlike the information gathered through directories and other sources, interviews can determine an association's motivations, experience, and attitude towards member services. The interview will represent a significant investment by your firm in time, personnel, and travel—be prepared.

Logistics

If all has gone well you have already identified the association executive, based on your research or response to your letter or survey. Your first call should be kept low-key and noncommittal for both parties. One scenario might be: "Mr/Ms. _____ , I have been given your name by _____ (this can be the association itself or, more impressively, a member) as the person in charge of services. Our company currently provides products (or services) that are utilized (or desired) by your members (if available, state usage statistics or a survey that proves member need or usage) and we are considering the potential advantages of working with a few selected associations in future marketing. Our research indicates that your association may be an ideal partner, and I was wondering whether you might have a few minutes to discuss this further (or, I will be in town next week and wondered what day might work best for your schedule)."

Assure your caller that the appointment will be kept to less than an hour and that, based on your knowledge of their membership, your product or service has significant potential. Once again the mentioning of your association participation (advertising, trade show, associate member) or, more importantly, your customers who are association members, can often make the difference. Frequent association objection is that the requested time conflicts with events, such as conventions, trade shows, and committee meetings. These objections are usually valid and your understanding will be welcome.

Attendees

Who should attend the interview? At a minimum, the person at your organization who is likely to develop and administer the program should be present. There is nothing more frustrating to the association than meeting different personnel at each meeting. Time is wasted bringing new parties up to speed, and the association is left to wonder if the vendor is organized adequately to support the program.

On the other hand, as your discussions move to a more serious stage, bringing in your senior management can be impressive—it exhibits your corporate commitment to the program. If you do enlist your senior management, make sure they are briefed about the association, the previous discussion, and the association's personnel in advance.

The Questions

Remember that the purpose of the interview is to determine the association's suitability for your product or service. The mission of the interview is to gather information, not sell or present a packaged proposal. If it is well-organized, the interview can lay valuable groundwork for the ultimate preparation of a proposal designed in response to the association's specified concerns and desires.

Depending on the quality of your directory and your background work, you may be able to answer some of the questions in advance and use the interview to confirm your impressions.

While you are not there to sell, you do want to plant a few seeds and build some credibility with the association. Therefore, before you begin the interview, you should present a brief corporate overview including your experience with the association's members and your financial backing and reiterate your interest in determining the potential advantages in working with an association. You may want to point out that you have chosen the association out of a large field because you believe it has the right membership and an excellent reputation. Caution: keep it short (5–10 minutes maximum)—you are there to interview the association.

What is the mission of your association? This answer simply defines the association and may provide you with information to better customize the proposal. An association is usually more comfortable with a product or service that is related to the association's mission and assists in its accomplishment.

When was your association organized and how has it changed? This question provides an open forum for association executives and may provide some insight as to their frustrations or ambitions. Usually, if services are a part of the association, they will be mentioned as part of the "changes."

How many members do you have and what is the membership trend? This question attempts to focus on the ever-present need to recruit new members and provides you further evidence of a growing or shrinking association. It is important to note that associations facing a consolidating membership may be your hungriest prospects, since the attraction of members and nondues income are critical for their survival.

How many potential members are there? Often as important as current members are the association's potential membership, since services are often used to attract nonmembers as well as to retain current members.

Who are the competitors for your members' dues? This question provides answers to two key questions: (1) Does the association face competition from other associations and therefore have a need to distinguish itself through services? and, just as important, (2) What other associations are available if this association says no? Keep in mind that the association's competitors may be national, state, local, or specialized associations.

What is the staffing of the association? This provides you with an idea of the staff available for assistance. You may wish to follow up with a specific question regarding the marketing and/or services staff.

Does the association have any for-profit subsidiaries? If so, what products or services does it now offer? This question will provide information on the current scope of activities. You may wish to follow up with a question regarding the program's penetration rate or success.

Does the association have any state or local affiliates and, if so, what is their relationship to your association? Local association affiliates may provide you additional support, but also remember that their membership may not be dual; members may only belong to one or the other. Also inquire if the local and national associations work together on services development and marketing.

Does the association have an annual convention, magazine, or newsletter? The answer confirms the association's marketing capabilities and is critical to your subsequent development of a marketing plan. If you are unfamiliar with these, you should also inquire whether the magazine and newsletter accept advertising and when the next convention is scheduled, since associations often prefer to roll out new services at their conventions.

Does your association seek nondues income and what are its largest contributors today? The answer provides additional information on the association's attitude toward services and its appetite for corporate partnerships.

What are the most important elements that the association considers as it reviews potential services? Associations have differing priorities; some will say increasing membership, revenue to the association, or savings or benefits to the membership. Regardless, these are critical elements for your proposal preparation.

Does the association have established sponsorship standards? As the experience of associations has expanded, many have adopted standards that programs must meet to be considered for the association's endorsement. Obtaining these standards prior to your submission can ensure that your proposal meets the association's basic requirements.

Does the association have a standard nomination or request-for-proposal form? Some associations have developed standard corporate nomination or request-for-proposal formats. These forms typically provide the association basic information regarding the vendor and should accompany your proposal, where applicable.

What is your decision-making process and what is the approximate time span from proposal to implementation? The question provides you a timetable for program development and reasonable expectations as to the process. A follow-up question: if the association states that a services committee reviews all proposals, when will the committee meet next? In some associations, service development is largely staff-driven and decisions can be made quickly, but in others the association depends on committee input and the timetable depends on the meeting schedule.

The Wrap-Up

If all has proceeded as you expected, wrap up the interview by stating that, based on the interview, you would like to prepare a proposal that the association can review. Emphasize that your selection of the association has been confirmed and that you are looking forward to a successful partnership. Indicate that you would like to draft the proposal for the association's review and comments before finalizing to ensure that it meets their needs. This assures the association that they will be provided input and weds the association to your efforts.

As you wrap up the interview it is important that you confirm the desired timing for a proposal, for if there is an upcoming meeting of the committee that reviews services, you may be able to expedite the association's consideration. In addition, ask for a copy of the association's magazine, newsletter, annual report, and membership recruitment package. These items will provide you an overview of the association's marketing, the relative importance of the areas you discussed, and fill in the gaps as you review the interview data.

THE BOTTOM LINE

Based on your own research, the use of tools of the trade and interviews, you have located the associations that meet your target needs; professional versus trade association, national versus state/local, and broad-based versus specialty. In addition, you can target associations that are motivated to build nondues income, provide member services, and attract and retain members. Now, you need to combine these elements and build a proposal that is too good to refuse.

NOTES

1. American Society of Association Executives, *Selling to Associations: Advice from Association Executives* (ASAE) p. 1.

Association Interview Worksheet
Name of the association _____ Date of interview _____

Address of association _____

Phone # _____ Fax _____
Association personnel interviewed:

Name _____ Title _____

Name _____ Title _____

Name _____ Title _____
Company personnel present:

Name _____ Title _____

Name _____ Title _____

Name _____ Title _____

The Questions

What is the mission of your association?

_____

_____

When was your association organized and how has it changed?

_____

_____

How many members do you have and what is the membership trend?

_____

_____

How many potential nonmembers are there and how do you recruit them?

_____

_____

What other associations compete for your members? Why do members join the other associations?

_____

_____

What is the staffing of the association? Specifically what staff supports the associations services and marketing?

_____

_____

Does the association have any for-profit subsidiaries? If so, what are its primary services?

_____

_____

Does the association have any state or local affiliates and, if so, what is their relationship to your association? Do they also offer member services?

_____

_____

_____

Does your association have an annual convention, magazine or newsletter? Does the magazine and newsletter accept advertising and articles of interest to the membership?

_____

_____

Does the association seek nondues income and what are its largest contributors? Why are these services successful?

_____

_____

What are the most important elements that the association considers as it reviews potential services? (Member needs; non-dues income; services that help attract and retain members, etc.)

_____

_____

Does the association have established sponsorship standards? If so request a copy of the standards to assure that your proposal meets the associations requirements.

_____

_____

Does the association have a standard nomination or request-for-proposal form? If so, request a copy.

_____

_____

What is your decision-making process and what is the approximate time-span from proposal to implementation? If a committee considers service proposals, when does it meet next?

_____

_____

The Wrap-Up

If the association meets your criteria, establish the timetable for the presentation of a proposal for the association's review. In addition, request copies of the association's magazine, newsletter, annual report, and membership recruitment package, for further review.

Chapter Eleven

A Proposal Too Good to Refuse

If your association interview accomplished its goal, your proposal will "write itself." The interview will have identified the association's mission, the role of nondues income, the importance of member services, and the key attributes by which a services program will be judged. Simply by listing these items, your proposal will be framed.

NOMINATION FORMS AND REQUESTS FOR PROPOSALS

While many associations rely on the corporate suitor to develop the proposal, others have established standard forms on which to base their submission. These forms, commonly called nomination or request-for-proposal (RFP) forms, delineate the key components of the association's evaluation and ensure that all vendors provide consistent data for staff and member evaluation; this is especially critical when more than one proposal for a similar program is being considered.

An awareness of the typical data requested can ensure that your proposal meets most association standards. For while many associations do not use standard forms, they nevertheless utilize many of the same criteria to review submitted proposals. While the content of nomination or RFP forms varies by association, most seek information in five areas: the proposed program, the provider, the product or services to be offered, the sales and marketing support, and financial data.[1]

The Proposed Program:

• What benefits will be provided to the membership? Benefits could include lower price, discounts, improved availability or access, simplified application or acceptance, or other unique characteristics.

• What are the sales, distribution, and fulfillment processes? Walk the association through the sales and delivery systems that members will encounter. Associations are particularly interested in how the corporation will be selling to its members: direct mail, corporate sales force, telemarketing, or independent sales organizations. Once the member has decided to purchase, how will the order be fulfilled, drop-shipped, or delivered and installed?

• What revenues and other benefits will the program provide the association? In addition to nondues income, benefits might include trade show attendance, event sponsorship, advertising, product usage, and input on further product development.

The Provider:

• Who are the corporation's principals and officers? Associations want assurance that the corporation's officers have the necessary experience to support the program as proposed. It is often useful to attach the biographies of key corporate people and emphasize their experience in working for or with members of the association.

• How long have they been in business? Discuss the corporation's experience, and, perhaps for new companies, include information on the principals' related experience to increase the association's comfort.

• What is the corporation's market share? If the program has been proposed to enable your company to penetrate an underserved niche (low market share), detail your research and demonstrate how the association program will help you increase market share; emphasize your previous success in penetrating other niches.

• What is the corporation's ability to support the association's membership response? If, for example, the corporation has only a small sales force, is it willing to expand based on membership response?

• Where are sales and service staff located? The association is seeking to ensure that the corporation's sales and support staff are located in areas that enable them to reach the majority of the membership. Providing the association a map of your sales and support locations is one solution.

• One area that many vendors overlook is the importance of the references and clients provided to the association. Remember that you are trying to increase the association's comfort in your capability and understanding of their market. Take time to review your client or reference list to make sure it is relevant to the association's membership. For example, if the association's members are small businesses, why provide a list of large employers or Fortune 500 companies?

• Will the corporation be able to continue to support the program financially? Don't overwhelm the association with financial data; provide a concise overview of the company's financial status. Often the inclusion of an annual report will suffice. For privately held companies, the provision of bank references may also be useful.

• Whom should the association call with questions regarding the proposal or the information provided? This contact should be an individual who has been involved in the process and, hopefully, was present during the interview of the association. Also include how the individual can be reached; phone, fax, and toll-free numbers are a must.

The Product or Services to Be Provided:

• Describe the service or products to be offered in your program. Unlike the description of the program, which included a brief overview of the products, this answer should detail the specific products to be offered. Copies of your marketing brochures can bring life to a dull list of product specifications.

• Will the program provide reduced prices and member discounts? The association seeks information on the savings the program will provide the membership. If your discounts are subject to further negotiation with the association, you may wish to include your current list prices and indicate a range of expected discounts, rather than commit to discounts that may be difficult to adhere to as negotiations proceed.

• How do the proposed products and pricing compare to your competition's and to those most commonly purchased by the association's membership. After all, while you may be offering a discount, the most commonly purchased product may already be priced significantly below your offer. The association is attempting to gauge the value of your offer.

Sales and Marketing Support

• What marketing support will be available to the program as proposed? Indicate the resources that will be employed to support the program, such as direct mail, telemarketing, advertising, sales force, public relations, and other promotional activities.

• What is your marketing plan? Using the resources detailed in the preceding question, detail how they will be deployed to market the program. Your marketing plan should be integrated with the resources and communication channels of the association.

Financial Information

• What are the members' purchase options? While many products will be purchased outright, other options might be available, such as leasing and rental. If these options are available to the association's members, they should be noted.

• How will the corporation report the results of the program to the association and at what frequency? Associations need to be aware of the program's progress and of sales to the members to track their income and the program's acceptance. Where possible, provide the association a sample of the reporting that would be used.

THE PROPOSAL COMPONENTS

While the standard submission forms of some associations ensure that basic information is provided, they tend to reduce even the most exciting proposals to clinical presentations. It is strongly suggested, therefore, that if an association has a nomination or an RFP that is to be accompanied by a proposal, that it presents your program in a concise and enthusiastic fashion. The proposal is your chance to tell your story; the nomination form of the association, if required, should be viewed simply as an appendix.

The proposal should highlight your desire to work with the association, discuss how the proposal will help the association meet its services, nondues income, and membership goals, and point out the advantages of your program to members versus nonmembers. It is important to keep in mind that corporate proposals are often circulated by association staff for member comment—so spend the time to prepare a proposal that reflects your professionalism and commitment.

The proposal is usually the first step in the association's decision-making process, not the last. Recognize that the proposal is a living document and that every effort should be made to seek and incorporate the association's input. Seek the association's thoughts by discussing early thoughts with staff, and fax a preliminary draft to the association for comments. There is no better barometer of member attitudes than the association's staff—keep them informed and leverage their knowledge. Strive to make your proposal a partnership, meeting both your needs and the association's. Perhaps the worst approach is one that signals to the association that the proposal is "take it or leave it"—they will likely leave it.

As you begin your proposal, think user-friendly; you are not drafting a legal treatise, but rather presenting an overview of your concept and discussing how it will benefit the association and meet its membership needs. Remember that an association seeks proposals that help solve problems, not create new ones. One of your key objectives is to exhibit your understanding of the association and your commitment to the program's success.

It is suggested that you limit your proposal to three pages and provide additional details, such as nomination or RFPs, in appendices if necessary. Longer proposals will tend to be skimmed and key points missed. There are six key components to an association proposal: an executive summary, a corporate profile, your membership or industry experience, the program overview, the marketing support, and the close.

An Executive Summary. This should appear on the first page and provide a summary of the proposal, emphasizing how the proposal would help the association meet its goals. For example, it may be appropriate to state, depending on the interview, "Our proposal has been developed in light of the interview conducted with the association. We believe the proposal offers the membership important discounts on first-quality products unavailable to nonmembers. We believe the program will provide the association with a vehicle to attract and retain members while building a solid source of nondues income. Our company is committed to the program through a marketing plan based on your association's communication channels and supported by our ongoing sales force and advertising efforts."

The executive summary should be based on the association hot-buttons elicited during the interview. The goal of the summary is to motivate the reader to complete the proposal.

A Corporate Profile. This gives evidence that your company has the stamina and the commitment to market, deliver, and support the program's products and services. The profile should provide financial information to indicate your company's solid footing, an overview of your product's market share, and examples of your commitment to quality, such as annual quality assurance surveys, product warranty experience, or your annual research budget.

The corporate profile is designed to assure the association that you have the ability to deliver on your promises and should increase the association's confidence that your program will be a success.

Referrals/Experience. Include an overview of your experience in working with the market represented by the association and a list of your membership referrals. This is also an opportunity to point out evidence of your existing support of the association, such as trade show exhibition, convention attendance, magazine advertising, or associate membership.

If your selection of the association was based on a referral of an association member, you should include a letter from the member that indicates member satisfaction with your services and explains how they may be useful to others. If, on the other hand, you have other association relationships, a letter from the association detailing how your corporation has delivered on its promises may also prove useful.

The Program. Summarize your offer. The section should include the products or services to be offered, the discounts or rebates available for members versus typical nonmember pricing, and the other features of the program. Vendors often hesitate to be specific in the draft proposal, preferring to await association reaction. But the draft proposal should, at a minimum, point out the potential advantages of such a program to generate adequate interest.

One area that often perplexes corporate partners is association revenue or royalties. After all, what is a reasonable royalty for the association's endorsement and access to its membership? Unfortunately, there is no common answer. The level of royalties is often based on the size of the potential market, the role of the association, the profit margin on the product offered, the competition, and the association's philosophy. Some associations seek services primarily to attract and retain members, while others build services to generate nondues income; their concepts of a reasonable level of royalty will therefore differ.

One approach worth considering is to discuss the royalty in the context of your overall offer and ask the association to suggest a reasonable level. For example, if you have estimated that access to the association's market may enable you to offer 20 percent off of list price, ask the association what percentage of the total 20 percent should be set aside for royalties. In programs in which discounts are not offered and the sale is based on increased access, such as insurance programs and financial services, royalties are usually viewed as part of what would normally be paid as marketing expenses.

A caution: if your proposal offers a specific royalty, be careful in estimating the association's revenues. Nothing can destroy your integrity faster than unrealistic sales and nondues income forecasts. Unrealistic expectations will curse your partnership from the start. Your proposal should be based on the results you have experienced elsewhere and on the previous experience of the association.

Marketing Support. A testimonial to your company's commitment to the program through use of the association's communication channels and your sales force and/or promotional efforts. Your proposal should highlight how your company will market and promote the program and reach the association's membership. One of the common association concerns is, "Can the company market and support the product for all the members?" For example, if you are courting a national association, you should discuss your nationwide sales force, regional support centers, or toll-free help lines. Remember, most associations do not want to offer products that are available to only a part of the membership. All members pay dues; therefore all members should be able to have access or, at a minimum, be able to apply for the services offered.

To exhibit your commitment to the association, you may also want to discuss the key elements in your marketing plan, such as association advertising, direct mail, trade show participation, sales force support, and toll-free member support lines. Offer the association an opportunity to develop a mutual marketing plan to ensure that all resources can be brought to bear. Remember that associations have limited marketing resources; therefore, point out any opportunities you may have to promote the program and the benefits of association membership, perhaps through your sales force or telemarketing department.

One popular way to kick-start your program is to offer the association's members a special introductory offer during the program's first 90 days. Such an offer can provide a catalyst to coordinate marketing efforts and often spurs strong sales. The limited time offer also provides an effective way to motivate and sell the sales force or telemarketing department on the value of the association program (see Chapter 14,The Marketing Plan).

The Close. The closing provides an opportunity to offer to further customize the program based on the association's and members' suggestions. This should include an offer to meet with members or committees to present the proposal and to finalize the program.

Before you wrap up the proposal, take the time to review your interview notes. Look for key association dates that might be used for the program's announcement or the next meeting of the committee that reviews service proposals. If either of these dates is within 90 days, you should refer to them and express your commitment to meeting them. Next, review your own marketing calendar. Does your product or service have a selling season, or is a new product announcement near? If so, let the association know and, once again, indicate your desire to have the program in place in time to take advantage of the selling season or to include new products.

The last paragraph should provide a quick snapshot of the program's benefits and your desire to ensure its success.

PROPOSALS–AN INSIDER'S VIEW

Associations receive countless unsolicited proposals from unheard of providers with unknown track records. The association executive is left with the task of determining which ones are worth pursuing. Here are some of the criteria used by an association:

1. Professionalism. Does the proposal indicate that the provider is a professional capable of making the program a success? It is amazing how many of the proposals received by an association executive are ill-prepared and lack even the basics, such as a phone number or address.

2. Relevancy. Many proposals are obviously mailed without attention to the association or its membership. Too often pro-

posals are rejected not because they are poor, but because they are simply irrelevant to the businesses or professionals represented by the association.

3. Timeliness. There are no bad ideas, just bad timing. Sometimes an association is simply overwhelmed with other business or a membership crisis, and proposals, good or bad, are ignored or shelved. This can be especially true in the months leading up to an association's annual convention or trade show or during a busy legislative session.

4. Need. Associations are looking for answers, and proposals that solve problems will get more attention. If, for example, an association is facing escalating insurance rates or a shortage of insurance carriers, it is more likely to listen to an insurance proposal than during soft market when prices are low and access easy. Pay attention to the problems that industries are facing; programs that solve problems, sell.

5. Commitment. Proposals are often judged by the resources and commitment the provider brings to the relationship. Does the company have the marketing capabilities and sales force necessary to sell the program and generate the desired results?

Regional, state, local, or start-up companies seeking the endorsement of a national association, without an adequate marketing commitment, are often viewed by associations as posing problems rather than offering solutions.

6. Understanding. Does the proposed partner understand the association? While the proposal may be directed at the correct target audience, it may reflect a poor understanding regarding the association's marketing capability, staffing, and motivations.

7. Value. Does the proposal offer the association's members a real value? Too often, an association proposal simply emphasizes the nondues income that it will generate and ignores the benefits to the membership. An association must pick and choose its partners with care, for each endorsement is an extension of its goodwill. If the members perceive that the association's services are association-driven, rather than membership-driven, future offerings will be increasingly ignored.

8. Implementation support. Is the proposal ready for implementation, or does it simply pose problems that will require endless staff time? Many so-called proposals are simply "what if"

inquiries. With limited staff available to flush out new services, staff will work with those who are ready to work with them.

9. Membership magnet. Is the offering proposed one that will attract and retain members? Likely this will be judged in light of what is already available to members and what new advantages the proposal will generate. Often the services that are the most critical in attracting and retaining members are not those that simply reduce prices but those that provide access to services or products unavailable without the members' collective buying or the association's assistance.

10. Nondues revenue. Generally if an association proposal provides member value and a vehicle for attracting and retaining members, it will, due to its success, provide a steady stream of nondues revenue. While royalties are not usually a primary motivator, they are considered if other criteria are met. Some proposals, however, ignore any reference to royalties, while others present exaggerated revenue projections that destroy the association's confidence in the proposal.

THE BOTTOM LINE

A partnership proposal should reflect the needs of the partners in an effort to accomplish mutual goals. The corporate partner seeks access to a targeted market of prospects that respects the association and the products it endorses. The association seeks to attract and retain members while building a source of nondues revenue.

A well-designed proposal is based on satisfying known association needs and building confidence in your ability to meet them.

PROPOSAL WORKSHEET

Reminder: proposals should be viewed as work-in-progress, and where possible they should be drafted in consultation with your association suitor. The more opportunities you provide for association input, the greater the odds that the association will become not only your partner but your advocate.

Keep your proposal to no more than three pages, for longer proposals tend to be skimmed and valuable points often overlooked. If necessary, provide additional information as appendices or attachments to your proposal.

I. The Executive Summary

The executive summary should appear on the first page and summarize the proposal, emphasizing how the proposal would help the association meet its goals. Remember, refer to the information you gathered in the interview of the association and target your proposal to satisfy the association's mission and program criteria.

_____

_____

_____

_____

_____

_____

II. A Corporate Profile

The corporate profile is designed to assure the association that you have the ability to support the proposed program, including its products, services, marketing, and member support. It is important to highlight your financial stamina, but don't overwhelm the association with numbers. Often this section can be supplemented by the inclusion of a corporate annual report, a report from a rating agency, or a market share analysis applicable to your industry.

_____

_____

_____

_____

_____

_____

_____

III. Referrals/Experience

This section is one of the most important, for it is your chance to showcase your experience with association members or your service to the association's industry. Your goal is to increase the association's comfort in your company and your experience in working with its membership and, where applicable, other associations.

If you include a list of referrals, check to see if they are association members or at least typical of the average association member. The more your referrals are related to the association, the more credible your experience is.

_____

_____

_____

_____

IV. The Program

The description of the proposed program should include an overview of the program, services, or products to be offered to the association's members. The section should include the specific products included in your offer and describe why you think they are relevant to the association's membership. You may wish to indicate that the program has been drafted on the basis of your knowledge of the association and express your willingness to further customize based on the needs of the association and its membership.

Caution: if your proposal includes a projection of the association's revenue, based on the program' usage, base your estimates on the penetration results of other association programs or on your experience with other associations. Unrealistic expectations will harm your credibility and set standards that may be very difficult to meet.

_____

_____

_____

_____

V. Marketing Support

The marketing support section seeks to answer three questions: How will you assure the program's success? What is your commitment to the program? What support are you expecting of the association?

Ideally, you should include a marketing plan that incorporates the resources of the corporation and the communication channels of the association.

_____

_____

_____

_____

_____

_____

VI. The Close

The proposal's closing section should be viewed as opening the door to further discussion and to the association's decision-making process. While the proposal will reflect significant effort, it should be viewed as basis for further negotiation.

Remember, many proposals are circulated among the members of the association, especially those on committees that review services. Be sure the close reiterates the member benefits your program will provide and your ability to support the program and its marketing.

_____

_____

_____

_____

_____

_____

Your proposal should be delivered or mailed to the association staff whom you initially met with.

NOTES

1. Mirlam Meister, "Marketing Sponsored Products and Services", *Marketing the Nonprofit Association* (GWSAE Foundation, 1992), p. 181.

Chapter Twelve

The Close

One area that perplexes and frustrates the for-profit sector is the decision-making processes of associations. After all, you have invested significant time and resources prospecting, interviewing, and proposing, yet no commitment has been received and certainly no deal has been closed. It is easy to understand the vendor's loss of patience, without an understanding of the decision-making process of an association and the vital role it fulfills.

THE DECISION-MAKING PROCESS

Associations are member driven; members are to an association what shareholders are to a corporation. But unlike shareholders, who may not be customers, members are both the association's "investors" and its customers. Therefore associations usually go to great lengths to solicit membership input as services are evaluated and approved. Such membership input provides the association valuable hands-on evaluation and usually ferrets out corporations who lack staying power and services that are simply passing fads.

The decision-making processes of associations will vary depending on the size and complexity of the association. The typical decision-making process involves three steps: staff review and evaluation, member review and evaluation, and association approval. The three steps can be accomplished within 90 days if the product is viewed as critical, to well over a year for projects given lower priority or requiring extensive research. Each of the steps provides the association with specific input and presents different challenges for the vendor.

Step 1–Staff Review and Evaluation

The first step in product evaluation is performed by association staff, usually in response to a vendor proposal or inquiry. The review by staff can encompass several meetings depending on the preparation of the vendor, the vendor's knowledge of the association, and the complexity of the product. The first meeting with staff is often the corporation's interview of the association, detailed in Chapter 10. While the association interview will usually provide significant guidance for the development of a proposal, it is amazing how often vendors will return for second and third interviews. Unfortunately, these subsequent interviews can be very frustrating to the association if valuable time is spent educating an ever-changing corporate cast. Such repetitious interviews only leave the association to wonder if the partner could deliver on any promise and certainly do not provide the association any incentive to expedite its decision making.

The time between the initial interview and the proposal's presentation should be no more than 60 days and ideally the proposal should be delivered to the association staff who attended the initial interview, since they are familiar with you, your company, and the advice provided during the interview. When presenting the proposal, emphasize that the proposal is still a draft and that you are seeking the association's input to refine it further. Point out that your program has been developed to satisfy the association's needs as identified in the interview and the needs of the association's membership.

Review the proposal with the staff. If attachments are included in the proposal, point them out, but unless requested avoid spending time in the details. Do take the time to review any letters of referral from satisfied member customers or from other associations.

If the association expresses interest, it will likely ask that the proposal be redrafted based on the discussion. The next step may be to meet again with staff to review the revised proposal or refer the proposal to the committee or members for review and recommendation.

At the staff interview, the most frequent objections will be related to your capability to support the program and the program's relevancy to the membership. While a strong proposal and association membership research can mitigate the concerns, an offer to conduct a test market may further alleviate association fears. Such a test market could encompass a sampling of the membership or the installation of products or equipment in test locations. Don't forget that the association may also be a user for the program. For example, if you are offering office equipment you could also provide the association with equipment.

Another alternative for determining member needs is to offer, in conjunction with the association, to conduct a survey of membership. A survey can often be accomplished quickly and the process will often tie the association more closely to the vendor. By offering to conduct the survey, vendors are also exhibiting both confidence and professionalism, both critical to the association's ultimate approval. If the product being considered is within a larger category of products, you might also suggest that the survey seek data on related subjects of interest to the association. For example, if your proposal involves a specific educational program, you could also inquire as to member usage of existing association educational offerings and their future educational needs.

An additional strategy, if staff skepticism is expressed, is to suggest that the proposal be forwarded to a focus group or small number of members for review. Remember that most staff are not experienced in the businesses or professions they are representing. Therefore the staff's view may be influenced by their limited understanding of member operations. The review by a focus group of the membership can only help you; without it, the proposal was likely dead in the water.

In addition, ask the staff, "If I could change one aspect of the proposal to help it meet the needs of the association and your members, what should it be?" If the response offers a constructive idea, ask if the association would be willing to reconsider the proposal after you incorporate the suggestions. If your efforts are still fruitless, ask the association to identify other potential associations. For often, while a program may not fit one association, it may be ideal for other associations that better represent your prospects or marketing capabilities.

Associations certainly do not make their decisions in haste, but, according to Karen Hoyt, of the American Dental Association, "Members look to the association and trust our recommendations. The bottom line is simple—our good name is our major asset, therefore we guard it—entry to our membership is not taken lightly."

Step 2–The Membership Review and Evaluation

If your proposal and perhaps subsequent revisions have passed the initial staff review, it will usually be forwarded to members for review. While some associations utilize small focus groups or fax polls, many refer proposals to an association committee for review. Corporations are usually asked to present their proposals at a committee meeting. You should view the committee presentation as your command performance, since it will likely be your only chance to present your proposal and, more importantly, exhibit your commitment to members of the association. The most important steps are preparing for the meeting and knowing your audience.

One of the biggest corporate oversights is failing to determine the composition and motivation of the committee. Often, vendors assume that the committee will simply "rubber stamp" the recommendation of the staff; however, the role of staff often changes when the proposal reaches the committee. Up to this point, staff has usually been your mentor, guiding your proposal's development. At the committee level, however, while staff provides the committee guidance, its advocacy is usually limited and the decision is left to the committee. After all, if the committee's members wouldn't participate, why would the rest of the membership.

The average committee consists of 15 members, usually composed of a cross-section of the association's membership.[1] Often vendors assume that the committees are composed of "typical" members and fail to take into account their specific needs and therefore biases. Understanding the composition of the committee's members enables you to tailor the presentation to address specific issues while de-emphasizing others. Knowledge of the group also permits presentations to highlight specific components of the proposal of interest to the committee. If, for example, you are presenting a health insurance program and the committee includes west coast members, you may want to highlight HMOs or PPOs, which are prevalent in the western states.

Some questions you should ask your staff contact as you prepare for the meeting of the committee include:

• How much time should the presentation take? Usually a company is provided one half-hour to two hours depending on the complexity of the proposal. It is important to keep to your allotted time and ask for questions from the committee members.

• Who would you suggest attend? The association will normally suggest that no more than two people attend so as not to overwhelm the committee. These should include the person who has been involved in the association discussions and a representative of corporate management. Management can often help to assure the association that the company is committed and provide quick answers to questions that would otherwise delay the program's approval. If you decide to invite senior management, make sure that they are familiar with the association, the proposal, and the composition of the committee.

• Does the committee prefer the use of slides, overheads, and videos? Generally audio-visuals help a meeting, but avoid videos that last longer than 15 minutes. The committee wants to meet you, not watch television. If you do use slides or overheads, provide the committee copies after your presentation.

• How many people will attend? It is important that you bring adequate copies of materials for the committee's review. All committee materials should be provided to staff in advance of the committee meeting. Staff will often review the materials and make suggestions based on previous meetings.

• Has the committee considered a similar program in the past? If so, what was the decision and why? Often staff can review copies of previous committee minutes and provide valuable insight on the committee's discussion and its concerns.

• Who are the members of the committee? Many vendors hesitate to ask the names of committee members and some associations are hesitant to provide a list, fearing the vendor will lobby members directly. Assure the staff that you are simply trying to tailor the presentation to the audience and that you will respect the confidentiality of the list. Useful data can include: the name, addresses, size of business, association services participation, and previous committee experience.

With the information in hand, determine: what specific products or services would appeal to the committee's members; if any of the members are already customers; and if your company has sales and service support in each of the member's regions or states. Your presentation can then be designed to highlight information that has been uncovered.

Remember that your audience now consist of members, not staff. Use your presentation to emphasize the member benefits of the program and the advantages of the program versus those available to nonmembers. Highlight your company's commitment to the industry and the program and detail how you will work to ensure its success—via your marketing plan. At committee meetings, many vendors emphasize the program's non-dues income potential and ignore the member benefits. Remember, unless the members are convinced of the program, the program will likely fail.

Normally your presentation will be followed by or include committee questions and objections. Most associations will permit the vendor to be present during early discussion, but will ask the company to leave during the committee's debate and decision making. If you sense or are informed of strong objections or skepticism, you may want to suggest conducting a test market or a survey to confirm member interest.

A committee will normally decide on one of three alternatives: approval of the program as presented, approval of the program pending the resolution of outstanding issues, or rejection of the program. The first two alternatives are good news; the third, rejection, presents several alternatives. First seek from staff the specific reasons for the rejection and inquire whether the reasons are viewed as curable and the proposal, therefore, worth a second try. Next, ask staff for suggestions of other associations that might be a market for the service or product. Association staff is often aware of other associations and may recommend that you pursue a local association or specialized association. Third, recognize that the process has provided you valuable insight on the needs of the membership and the marketing assistance available from the association. Target your future marketing to increase association and member awareness through conventions, trade shows, associate membership, and advertising (see Chapter 14).

Step 3–Association Approval

Once your proposal has been approved by the association's committee, the committee usually recommends approval by the association's executive committee or board of directors. It is rare that the association withholds approval once the committee has acted. However, it is strongly recommended that if the committee's approval was conditional, outstanding issues be resolved quickly. Usually companies are not asked to present their proposal to the executive committee or board, since the association's leadership depends on the recommendation of the committee and the work of staff.

THE MARRIAGE CONTRACT

Your dating is now complete and you are ready to write the marriage vows to seal a long-term association partnership.

NOTES

1. *Policies and Procedures in Association Management*, p. 21.

Chapter Thirteen

The Agreement

The purpose of agreements is to frame the duties and responsibilities of each party, but often in the process of negotiation and presentation, roles change, or worse, become confused. Before the agreement is drafted, a simple matrix can provide each party with a clear view of the program and the lawyers with a summary on which to base the contract and, later, aid the development of the marketing plan. The matrix should list the program's major duties and identify who is responsible for each.

Program Matrix: XYZ Program

Company	Association
Appoints program manager	Appoints program manager
Develops advertising	Approves advertising
Develops member marketing kit	Approves kit and mailing
Drafts corporate press release	Drafts member press release
Conducts sales force orientation	Attends sales orientation
Responds to member inquirers's	Refers inquiring members
Accepts orders or enrollments	Notified of rejections
Ships orders and bills	Quarterly sales update
Updates member lists	Provides member lists
Attends convention	Notifies of convention
Responds to complaints	Notifies of problems
Develops new products	Approves new products

Once the parties have agreed on the matrix, contract work is simplified because many program operational issues have been resolved. The final contract will provide not only the program's legal framework, but, along with the matrix, should be viewed as a living document to guide the parties through the program's implementation and operation.

The association's approval is contingent on the drafting of an acceptable agreement. Often, vendors assume that since the proposal has been accepted the association will simply sign on the dotted line. The problem is that most vendors attempt to utilize agreements that were originally drafted for use with for-profit companies, such as licensing or bulk purchasing agreements. While these agreements often contain provisions that will be included in the association's agreement, they often lack provisions necessary to protect the association's tax-exempt status, limit its liability, protect its ownership and control of the program, and clearly define the responsibilities of each party.

Before you begin to draft an agreement, inquire whether the association has a standard agreement or wants to prepare its own agreement. Association agreements with vendors contain provisions that are often unfamiliar to corporations, and using the association's form can often save the vendor significant time and legal costs.

KEY COMPONENTS

While each association agreement will differ depending on the complexity of the program, most agreements contain ten major components:

Name of the program. Many times the program's name is ignored and valuable marketing is wasted. The program's name should incorporate the association's name or logo and identify the vendor or the key products or services to be offered. If, for example, you are working with ABC association to offer fax machines you might select a name like ABC Fax Program, or, if the product line is likely to be expanded, a broader name like ABC Communications Program could be used.

Adopting of a unified program name permits you to market your products with the name and goodwill of the association. Each time you advertise, your name is associated with the association. In addition, some associations will require that all endorsed vendors display a standard "seal of approval" in association advertising. The seal is designed to make members aware of the association's endorsement or sponsorship. The association may require the seal in addition to the adoption of a program name or in lieu of a program name.

Remember that an association program provides access to the association's membership; therefore, anything that increases the program's visibility and therefore credibility is worth fighting for. The program's name is a good place to start.

Eligibility. Who will be eligible to participate in the program? While it is likely that only association members will be able to purchase or participate, some associations may wish to include members of local chapters or affiliates. The more potential customers that can be targeted, the greater the odds of success. Such membership extensions benefit both parties.

Responsibilities of the corporation. This section establishes the responsibilities of the corporation and the resources that will be dedicated to the program and its marketing. Responsibilities may include: the provision of toll-free phone numbers for member inquiries and orders; a pledge to respond to member requests and information diligently and expeditiously; and/or a commitment to advertise in the association's publications and exhibit at the association's trade show.

Most associations will require the vendor to assume all responsibility for all matters related to the sale of its goods or services, including accepting orders, billing, collection, delivery, service, and warranty. The association often will require this to limit its liability and, in some cases, to meet requirements related to its tax-exempt status or other tax-related needs.

It is important to state which party is responsible for the program's operation, underwriting, or member acceptance. It is also strongly suggested that the company name a "program manager"—an individual responsible for the program's implementation and operation. While the named individual may not actually perform all required functions, the program manager is the liaison between the company and the association. The position is critical, for once a program has been launched, the individuals involved often move on to other assignments or accounts. Unless one individual is held responsible for the program, the agreement may signify the end, rather than the beginning, of a relationship.

Responsibilities of the association. This section establishes the responsibilities of the association. Since most associations are simply endorsing the program, they will usually commit to three specific responsibilities: to use their best efforts to endorse the program to members, to cooperate with your marketing and promotion of the program, and to employ regular membership communications to make members aware of the program and its benefits. Remember that for the association's revenue to be treated as royalty income, the association's role must be limited to the licensing of its name, not the exchange of goods or services such as complimentary advertising space, free booth space, or postage for program mailings. Simply put, an association commits to providing access, but it is clearly up to you to take full advantage of it.

While most associations limit their marketing assistance, some associations are willing to perform more specific marketing functions to support the program. Because of their larger staffs and in-house marketing expertise, these associations can often provide a vendor an alternative marketing and distribution channel.

In either case, it is critical that you fully understand the association's available communication channels to ensure their full utilization. Ideally the promotion of the association should compliment and reinforce your sales and marketing efforts. One option is develop a joint marketing plan, separate from the agreement, to establish a promotional timetable and define mutual expectations (see Chapter 15, The Marketing Plan).

It is also suggested that the association appoint an individual as its program manager. The association's program manager would work in conjunction with the appointed corporate program manager to ensure that the program marketing plans are implemented and that program issues are quickly resolved.

The products/services. This section provides a description of the products or services that are included in the program.

For programs that encompass a menu of products or services, this section can be supplemented by an appendix to the agreement that details the specific program components. It is also important to note those items not included in the program, such as other products offered by the company.

You may also want to include a provision to permit you to add or delete products from the program. Normally the association agrees to the provision as long as reasonable notice is provided and new items are subject to the association's approval.

Association revenue. Income to the association is generally based on the sale or usage of your program or product. It is strongly recommended that an incentive-based system be adopted, which increases as sales increase. Such a formula will keep both parties wedded to the marketing plan and simplify future negotiations and extensions of the agreement. It is critical that the agreement include all components of the formula in one section and that the association clearly understands how it will be calculated. To avoid future disputes it is strongly suggested that an example of the formula's calculation be included within the contract or in an appendix to the agreement.

The results of your marketing and the association revenue produced should be reported to the association frequently, but some corporations prefer to distribute income only on a quarterly or semi-annual basis to maximize impact and minimize administrative costs. Your agreement should specify when the revenues will be reported and paid.

While most associations who perform limited marketing functions will prefer that the revenues be defined as royalties, other associations, who have agreed to perform more specific marketing support, may wish to identify those functions and have them identified as administrative or marketing fees.

Be careful to list exclusions to the revenue calculation, such as returned items, shipping charges, postage, interest on installment sales, and items not included in the program.

Marketing/advertising. Most associations will insist that all vendor marketing materials that refer to the association or display its name or logo be approved in advance by the association. The provision permits the association to review copy in order to ensure that its endorsement is being applied only to program products and not being extended to unrelated services or products of the company.

It is also suggested that companies seek approval for association marketing that features the vendor's program. While the association will not advertise the program, it often will include the program in membership marketing materials, publications, or press releases. Corporate review is especially important for insurance programs and other programs where acceptance is conditional and policy language therefore critical.

While some feel such approvals delay marketing, they are necessary to protect the partnership and can be accomplished quickly via fax and overnight mail.

Indemnification. The indemnification provision is often a major hurdle to an association agreement. The association will usually insist on total indemnification for any and all acts related to the program and its products, while the vendor often seeks more restrictive indemnification or cross-indemnifications. Associations are reluctant to indemnify since in most programs they perform few, if any, active roles and therefore are not responsible for a program's operation.

A compromise often agreed to is to indemnify the association for the operation of the program, except for actions taken by the association without the permission or agreement of the vendor, such as marketing or promotional misstatements. Associations may also require that indemnification be insured and that a copy of the applicable coverage be attached to the agreement.

Relationship of the parties. While you and the association are establishing a marketing partnership, most associations will require that the agreement clearly state that the program does not create a legal or business partnership or joint venture. Such a statement is important to the association, for it reiterates that the role of the association is limited to the provision of intangible assets, rather than performing active functions such as marketing or billing.

Term. Associations generally favor short agreements, especially with new programs. Short-term agreements permit the association to test the vendor and limit its risk if the program fails. A compromise is a one- or two-year agreement that automatically renews unless one of the parties provides notice. This option can be very effective if the royalty is incentive-based, since it can almost eliminate the need for costly renegotiation.

However, in programs where both parties acknowledge that success will require long-term commitment, such as insurance and financial services programs, longer term agreements should be sought. Such agreements provide the corporate partner the assurance of association support and the association assurance that the provider is committed to the program. If the association hesitates to execute a longer term agreement, one option is to develop a series of marketing goals or quality assurance standards, upon which the contract's renewal would be contingent. The agreement could then provide that if the goals or standards are not met, the agreement could be terminated with reasonable notice. Such a provision can also be an effective tool to keep the association's "feet to the fire," since the termination provisions can usually be made mutual.

Termination. One of the most overlooked sections of an agreement is the termination provision; after all, no one wants to talk about divorce during the courtship. The termination provision should address who can terminate the agreement, under what circumstances or conditions, and whether the conditions can be triggered with or without "cause." If cause is required, the agreement should also define the cause, the amount of notice required, the time provided to cure the breach, and, as important, the dispute resolution system.

The goal of an effective dispute resolution provision is to avoid any premature terminations and litigation. The most common resolution provisions found in association agreements are head-to-head meetings, perhaps between the program managers, by the appointment of a special committee, or through arbitration or mediation.

STICKING POINTS

While many agreements will be completed quickly, others will confront hurdles that may baffle and surprise the unsuspecting corporate partner. Most of the sticking points will encompass the treatment of existing business and issues related to the payment of association income:

- Existing business. Since most vendors will seek out associations that represent their existing customers or prospects, it is likely that some of your customers will be association members. The association is likely to ask whether you are willing to permit your existing customers who are already association members to take advantage of the proposed program. While the vendor may resist passing on discounts to existing customers, the association will point out that those members have paid dues and therefore should be able to receive agreed-upon discounts.

Passing on association discounts will normally present no problem for companies that offer single purchase products, such as supplies and equipment, since each purchasing decision is independent. However, the issue is far more complicated for services which require an ongoing commitment or long-term contract, such as data processing or insurance programs.

One option is to permit existing customers who are association members to roll over to the association program pricing as their agreements terminate. Another option is to offer the association pricing to those accounts added within the last six months, since these members will be most likely to seek an adjustment in their current pricing once the association's program is announced.

- Royalties paid on existing business. The association may also ask that the corporate partner pay royalties on existing business generated by association members. While some corporations may resent associations seeking income from their existing business, others view the request as an opportunity. One option, is to pay royalties on "old" business only to the extent that the association generates "new" business. Therefore, the association has an additional incentive to support the implementation of the program's marketing plan.

• Royalty formulas. Often, companies will attempt to negotiate an income payable to the association only after the company program reaches specific marketing targets. The
company will argue that such a formula is reasonable, since it
needs to recover its costs of program development, including
the discounts offered, before it can afford to share income with
the association. Associations, on the other hand, will point out
that the responsibility for marketing, and therefore the results,
depend largely on the company's marketing and sales efforts,
not the association's, and therefore contingent payment obligations are unacceptable.

An incentive-based formula can provide companies a
method to initiate payments, while limiting expenses, during
the start-up period of the program.

• Continuing association royalties. Associations are often
concerned that once corporate partners reach their desired
penetration level, they may withdraw their support in order
to eliminate the need to pay the association. Therefore some
associations will require that agreements contain a continuing
income provision. While these provisions are most commonly
used in association insurance programs, they are being incor-
porated into a variety of other endorsement agreements.
While most companies have no intent to discontinue successful programs, continuing income provides the association
with a financial cushion and the company, a disincentive to
terminate the relationship.

Continuing income provisions often become a very emo-
tional negotiating issue. Often, the company feels that, in requiring the provision, the association is doubting its integrity
and intent. The association, on the other hand, has seen companies come and go and its request is likely based on previous
poor experiences. Rather than let your emotions take over,
concentrate on the conditions of the provision and what events
would trigger the payment of fees. For example, if you did
decide to terminate the program's support, you may not mind
paying the association a fee if the association does not endorse
any other provider. You might also agree to the payment of
continuing fees if you breach on the terms of the agreement,

but you may want to provide that if the association fails to perform, the fees would be waived or reduced.

• Exclusivity. Some associations may require suppliers to agree not to offer a similar program to other associations that represent the same membership. The association's concern is that, if the program is offered to their members through other associations, the value of the program will be diminished. Suppliers are often concerned that such a provision limits their expansion capabilities, but if the provision is drawn narrowly, perhaps by naming those prohibited associations, agreement may not be difficult.

Corporate suitors, on the other hand, often seek exclusivity from the association to ensure that the association does not endorse another provider of the same products being offered. Since the association has chosen to endorse the vendor, exclusivity is not usually a problem, so long as the provision encompasses only those products of the company that are included within the program.

• Program performance data. It is not uncommon for associations to require that partners provide information on the program's performance. While most information will cause little concern, such as information detailing program sales by product line or by state or association region, other information may be viewed more critically. Some associations may also request information on the program's profitability or the company's marketing expenses, information that some view as confidential.

Generally information on profitability is limited to insurance programs and other programs where the association's program is viewed as a separate profit center. The sharing of such data can often be used to justify additional association marketing and support, since few programs will be profitable in the early years. The data can also provide the association with a clear picture of a corporation's commitment to the program and increases its willingness to ensure its long term success.

To ensure that information is used only to benefit the program and its marketing, you should also include a provision stating that all information is confidential.

EXECUTION

All too often, companies treat the execution of an agreement as the culmination of their long efforts, since many companies will have invested 6 to 12 months of time, personnel, and resources. Often, rather than view the agreement as a catalyst and road map for implementation and marketing, the company sees it as an excuse to move on to the next association or prospect.

However, the execution of an association agreement, unlike a sales contract, does not guarantee the receipt of revenue or the booking of orders—the results depend on your implementation and marketing. The time to start is now.

ASSOCIATION AGREEMENT CHECKLIST

Name of the program. Has a name been chosen for the program that incorporates the name of the association and identifies the vendor or the key products or services to be offered?

Eligibility. Is it clear who will be offered access the program, such as members, associate members, state or local chapter members, or related groups?

Corporate responsibilities. Have the responsibilities of the corporation been clearly defined and do they encompass the duties included in the program matrix?

Association responsibilities. Have the responsibilities of the association been clearly defined and do they encompass the duties included in the program matrix?

Products/services. Have the products and services to be included in the program been listed within the agreement or an appendix to the agreement? Are both parties clear as to the products or services excluded from the program?

Association revenue. If the association's revenue is to be based on a formula, does the agreement define all the components of the formula and provide an example of the required calculation? Does the agreement identify those items which are excluded from the revenue formula?

Marketing and advertising. Does the agreement provide that each party must obtain approval of the other party before using the program's name or party's name to ensure that the program's marketing is consistent with the agreement?

Indemnification. Are the parties clear on what actions are indemnified, and, if required, has the necessary insurance been obtained?

Relationship of the parties. Is it clear that the agreement does not establish a business or legal partnership or joint venture?

Term. Regardless of the initial term of the agreement, does it provide for the resolution of disputes that may arise during its operation?

Termination. If the contract provides for early termination, does it clearly state under what conditions and with what notice the termination could be activated?

Chapter Fourteen

The Marketing Plan

A program has now been developed that meets member needs, adds membership value, builds a nondues revenue stream, and enables products or services to be marketed with the clout of an association respected by its membership.

Yet, despite such efforts, the partnership will fail—if you fail to market. For while you have harnessed the endorsement of the association and gained powerful access to its membership, leveraging the newly found clout is the corporate partner's responsibility and challenge. As in politics, the first 100 days of any program are critical to its success, for the program's launch exhibits to both the membership and the association your commitment and expectations. For association marketing to succeed, it must be a joint effort of the association and the partner. The partnership's marketing should piggy-back on the association's communication channels and compliment the promotional and sales efforts of the corporate suitor. Marketing that fails to leverage the resources of both parties will be ineffective and inefficient.

Before launching headlong into an advertising and promotional blitz, let's review the objectives of the marketing plan:

• To promote the endorsement of the association. Most associations commit to support the marketing of the partner. To ensure that the association's endorsement is actively promoted, a well-designed marketing plan ensures that sales, advertising, and promotional efforts are integrated into those of the association.

• Build member confidence in the association's selection process. One of the key benefits of endorsed programs is the ability to raise the buying confidence of members and shortcut the decision making. Marketing efforts need to emphasize the association's evaluation and selection process and, more importantly, must emphasize why the corporation and its products or services were selected for the association's exclusive endorsement.

• Exhibit your corporate commitment. Members want assurance that they are buying from a company that understands their business or profession and is committed to their long-term success. In these uncertain times, the association's endorsement provides members added buying confidence.

• Associate your company with the association. When members think of the association, they should also think of your company or program. By leveraging the marketing resources of the corporate partner and the association, your message can be fully integrated into the association's communications and culture.

THE CAPABILITIES OF THE ASSOCIATION

As you begin to design your marketing plan, examine the association's marketing capabilities and resources. If the association has communication channels available, marketing can then be targeted and the partnership's resources leveraged. Based on your research and interview of the association, some of the association's capabilities may have been uncovered. Now is the time to confirm the specific tools available and the limits of their usage.

Membership data. What is the quality of the association's membership data? What membership information does the association compile regarding its members? For example:

Geographic data. Associations can usually identify members by state, region, and zip code. This information is critical to target marketing, sales, and promotional efforts. The data, when cross-referenced with corporate information, may also assist in identifying specific product or service needs.

Demographic data. Many associations also have the ability to identify members based on the size of their businesses, since often dues are based on similar data. In addition, through members surveys or other industry data, the association may also be able to identify other, more specific, criteria.

Corporate data. Many associations can also segment their membership by titles or functions. This information can prove very useful in targeting mailings within a business or profession. In addition, associations are increasingly dividing their membership into small segments, often called sections or councils. These association subgroups offer an additional opportunity to target market.

Prospective members. In order to solicit for membership, most associations maintain lists of prospective nonmembers. Since services often provide a mechanism for attracting nonmembers, they also provide the vendor an additional target audience.

Service users. Members who are current users of the association's services are likely to be strong prospects for the purchase of additional services. Determine if the association can compile a list of members who are frequent buyers of the association's services. Your mailings can then be targeted and customized to reflect the member's loyalty. Most associations also retain lists of members who have attended association seminars or other educational programs. These lists enable you to target prospects with specific interests. For example, if an association sponsors a seminar on retirement planning, attendees may be excellent candidates for financial services; if the association sponsors a seminar on industry automation, the attendees may be a receptive market for software, hardware, or specialty equipment programs.

If the association's membership information is limited, inquire whether the association can provide the data in a format that would enable you to manipulate or cross-reference it with other industries, corporate data, or your customer list.

Mailing assistance. Associations may prefer to mail program materials and bill the partner for the service. This permits the association to check the mailing's content, approve its use of the association's name and logo, and coordinate the distribution to avoid member mail glut. Other associations prefer that companies handle their own mailings and simply require that they approve the package prior to distribution.

Association name/logo usage. Determine the association's policy regarding the use of its name and logo on marketing materials. By obtaining the association's camera-ready advertising or logo "slicks", your task will be simplified. Also check to see if the association prefers the use of a tag line after its name, such as, "XYZ Association . . . serving America's industry."

Association magazine. Confirm that the association produces a magazine and determine its frequency and whether it accepts advertising. Next determine the magazine's deadlines for advertisements and its lead times and guidelines for article submissions. Remember that some associations also produce specialized journals or magazines for certain segments of the association's members. These publications may enable articles and advertising to be further segmented.

Newsletters. Check whether the association produces membership newsletters, their frequency, and if they accept advertising. Larger associations may produce several newsletters that address different specialties and therefore present additional marketing opportunities. Inquire if the newsletter accepts articles, acquire the applicable submission guidelines, and determine lead time.

Although some newsletters will not accept advertising, some associations may be willing to include advertising inserts or press releases in their newsletters to promote endorsed services. These inserts are a powerful marketing tool since they are usually limited to endorsed vendors and thus advertising glut is avoided.

Press releases. Determine if the association sends out press releases and to whom they are sent. An association's press releases will usually target industry or professional periodicals, its membership, and, less often, the general public. The association's press list can often compliment that of the corporate partner to ensure the broadest audience for the program's announcement.

Credit card statements. Does the association sponsor an affinity credit card for its membership? Often the credit card statements can be inserted with association information and new program offerings. Since the card is carried by members that believe in and want to support the association, they are likely to be strong prospects for other association services.

State associations/affiliates/sections. Does the association have state or local chapters or affiliates and what is their role in marketing or promoting the association's services? If these chapters or affiliates offer additional support for the association's programs, marketing should include efforts to increase their awareness and encourage their promotion and support locally.

The association may also have sections or councils which represent sectors or specialties within the association. These association sections may provide an additional opportunity for marketing and promotional efforts.

Conventions/trade shows. What conventions and trade shows are scheduled? Attendance and exhibition should be integrated into the marketing plan and promotional efforts. Conventions can attract over 30 percent of an association's membership—a significant marketing opportunity that should not be overlooked. It is important to note that many associations now hold multiple trade shows and conventions that are often targeted at various sectors of their membership. Therefore each of the association's trade shows or conventions may represent an opportunity to further target your message and promote specific program components.

Association publications. Associations often publish membership directories, educational catalogs, pamphlets, and association calendars. These publications may provide an opportunity for additional exposure through advertising or their sponsorship. These publications often provide a good value, since they usually permit only limited advertising and have a longer shelf life than newsletters or magazines.

THE P.A.S.S. SYSTEM

An association marketing plan consists of four integral elements: Promotion; Advertising; Sales and Support. Each of these components utilizes resources of both the corporate partner and the association.

Promotion

The program's success will be largely based on the ability to integrate the goodwill and communication channels of the association with the expertise of the corporate partner. Effective association promotion combines the clout of the association and the resources of the corporate partner. Program promotion includes the initial offer, press releases, magazines and news letters, direct mail, conventions and trade shows, and telemarketing.

The offer. Like all prospects, association members, face a mail and information glut that can undermine almost any promotional efforts. Therefore the first component of an effective promotional campaign is the design of the initial offer. A well-designed offer will provide a shotgun start to the program and will act as a catalyst for a coordinated promotional campaign. The goal of the offer is to provide members with an incentive to act now, rather than later. Initial offers can include:

A charter enrollment period. Charter periods are limited-time offers to recognize early program participants. During the charter period, members might receive extra discounts, product enhancements, reduced enrollment requirements, or a premium that recognizes their support of the program. To be effective, these offers should have limited "open windows" not exceeding 90 days. The use of a limited offer focuses the marketing efforts of both parties.

Introductory pricing. Reduced pricing on the product menu for a limited period of time introduces the program to the membership. The pricing could be an extra discount on all products offered or simply a discount on a few select but highly used products.

Open seasons. Some products or services have a distinctive buying season, and using an open-season purchasing window can focus marketing and reduce membership inertia. While insurance programs are the most frequent users of open seasons, many other products and services, in which buying is concentrated within narrow time frames can take advantage of this membership marketing technique.

Special financing. For a limited period, members may receive special financing or leasing terms. This can generate sales that may have waited till members had necessary money to purchase and also offers an alternative to reducing price.

Premiums/rebates. During the program's launch, members could be provided an opportunity to receive premiums or rebates based on purchases. The rebates might be in the form of coupons that could be applied to the purchase of additional products or services, while the premium's value could be based on purchased volume.

Press releases. All too often, a press release is viewed as simply a method to notify the press of corporate announcements. In fact, a press release is a promotional tool that can inform and motivate prospects. The key is to recognize that there are several audiences for a press release, each one representing a unique promotional opportunity.

First, press releases should be employed by both the association and the partner to notify their respective audiences of the program's development. The corporate partner notifies the press and the investment community, while the association notifies the trade press, usually composed of magazines and newsletters read by the association's members and nonmembers. These press releases announce the partnership's formation and emphasize the advantages to the association and the partner.

Press releases also provide a low-cost method to promote the program to additional audiences. Since press releases are usually viewed as news, they are a low-cost, high-response alternative to traditional advertising and direct mail. The two most overlooked audiences for press release are the members of the association and the company's sales force and support staff.

Sent to the association's membership, a press release provides a highly visible announcement that can ease the way for follow-up marketing. By including a reply card, readers can easily seek additional information and a prospect list can be assembled. The corporate press release, on the other hand, can be directed to the company's sales force and support staff to introduce the program, confirm the corporation's commitment, and announce the program's implementation date. There is nothing worse than a sales force that is unaware of a program or a support staff that is unable to respond to member questions—a press release can inform and prepare a sales force and support staff.

Association magazines and newsletters. When we think of promotional opportunities in magazines and newsletters, we often think of advertising, but for association publications such thinking is far too narrow. Often one of the only connections between the association and its members are its magazine and newsletters, for, unlike conventions and trade shows, they reach every member. Any promotional campaign should incorporate the full menu of available support:

Articles. Most associations welcome articles announcing a new program or service of the association. Such articles can provide an excellent introduction to the program and, unlike an advertisement, can detail the program's advantages. Program articles should be written for the membership and where possible should include examples of how specific members have used the program and how the program helps members meet their business or professional goals.

Once the program is launched, periodic magazine or newsletter articles regarding the program's success, member usage, and program enhancements can keep the program in front of the membership. Once published, the articles can be reprinted and used effectively in sales kits and direct mail.

Magazine columns. Association magazines may be willing to accept a monthly column concerning industry trends that may affect the membership, which will indirectly promote your program's benefits. Such columns provide the association's membership with a valued service, give your program heightened visibility, and provide the association with tangible evidence of your ongoing commitment.

Periodic announcements. Add the association's magazine to your corporate press release list. Even if most of the information goes unused, the releases keep your name in front of the editor and the association.

Direct mail. Most direct mail efforts are wasted because they fail to utilize the goodwill of the association and therefore are perceived as junk mail. You have worked hard for the association's endorsement—take advantage of every available opportunity.

Association branding. Explore whether the association is willing to send your mailing in its envelopes or permit you to add its name to your envelopes. In addition, the association may permit you to use its letterhead in your direct-mail package. Association branding provides a powerful method to separate your message from junk mail.

The mailing. Many associations are willing to handle the distribution of your direct mail. While the association will usually pass its costs to the vendor, association mailings ensure that current mailing lists are used and that the mailing does not conflict with other association mailings.

Keep it simple. Direct mail is intended to raise interest levels and provide members an opportunity to request further information. The most successful mailings are usually those that are kept to one page, provide the reader with a snapshot of the product or service, and include several response options, including postage-paid reply cards, toll-free 800-numbers, and fax numbers.

Alternative direct mail. While the direct-mail package is almost an institution, other methods have shown solid results. With the increasing popularity of fax machines, broadcast fax can deliver product or service information at very low cost. Many associations have the fax numbers of members and a few are already using broadcast fax for political updates and lobbying.

Postcards are another interesting alternative to direct mail. While many think that postcards are too small to carry an effective message, the post office accepts postcards that measure up to 4½'' × 11½''. While first-class postage rates are charged for any postcard in excess of 3½'' × 5½'', larger postcards are an excellent medium for announcing limited-time offers or new products, or reminding members of previous direct-mail offers.

Overnight or express mail is increasingly becoming viable alternatives to traditional first-class mail. Overnight mail distinguishes your package from other mail and demands to be opened first.

Conventions/trade shows. Conventions and trade shows are one of the most efficient ways to reach your targeted audience. According to the Trade Show Bureau, the cost of obtaining a business contact at a trade show is less than half the cost of business call, and, more importantly, leads generated at trade shows cost 70 percent less to close than field sales calls; due to the reduced number of sales calls required to close the sale.[1] Your success at association trade shows and conventions, however, will not be judged by your mere presence, but by how you take advantage of the many opportunities to promote your company and your association program.

Expositions. One of the main features of conventions and trade shows is the exhibit hall, which showcases products and services of interest to the association's membership. Association expositions offer companies the opportunity to generate corporate and program awareness, introduce new products, display new applications, provide customers access to company experts, attract media attention, expose employees to the industry's leaders, and signal your support of the industry that you are selling.[2]

The keys to exhibition success are to build booth traffic and ensure that attendees recall your exhibition. Most of the work, therefore, will take place before the show opens, in the design of the booth and preshow activities. Preshow promotional activities have proven to increase booth traffic by 33 percent, according to a survey conducted by the Trade Show Bureau. For while the association will promote the show and its exhibitors, most attendees learn of the show and of specific exhibitors through advertisements in trade publications and exhibitor announcements.[3] Inquire whether the association provides a list of registered members and announce your exposition participation and the benefits of your program.

While the size of the exhibit does influence the impression of visitors, other factors contribute to visitor recall, including product interest, live demonstrations, exhibit color/design, booth staff, literature availability, and knowledge of the company (see Exhibit 14–1).

To maximize booth traffic, select space in consultation with the association, for some associations group endorsed vendors and others provide preferred or advanced booth-space selection to selected vendors. One option is to locate near those booths that have traditionally generated high traffic or other successful association products or services; often the success, or, at least, the traffic, will rub off.

While most company booths display the corporation's logo or products, they often ignore the value of promoting the association's endorsement or, at a minimum, the association program's name. Therefore members visiting the exhibit hall have no way of distinguishing vendors that have earned the association's endorsement from other exhibitors. By working with the association to develop signage that exhibits your association affiliation and shouts your endorsement, recognition and traffic increase.

EXHIBIT 14–1
Reasons Other Than Size for Remembering an Exhibit

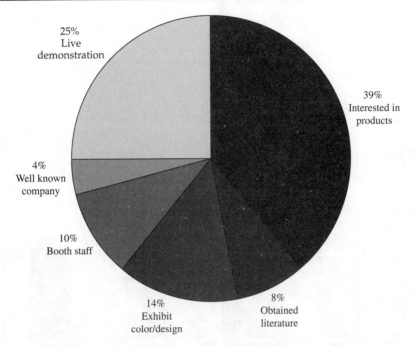

From the Trade Show Bureau, © 1992. Used with permission.

Make sure that the people who manage your booth are familiar with the association program, not simply with the company's products. All too often, the person minding the booth is unfamiliar with the details of the program and sales opportunities are lost. In fact, according to the Trade Show Bureau, 32 percent of trade show attendees intending to make a purchasing decision can cite at least one example (other than price or product performance) of holding back their order because of poor sales interaction. The largest single factor cited by trade show attendees was their impression that the salesperson didn't understand their needs.

While the average booth space rental is only $11 per square foot, your exhibition will also represent a significant investment

EXHIBIT 14–2
Why Customers Don't Buy from Exhibitors

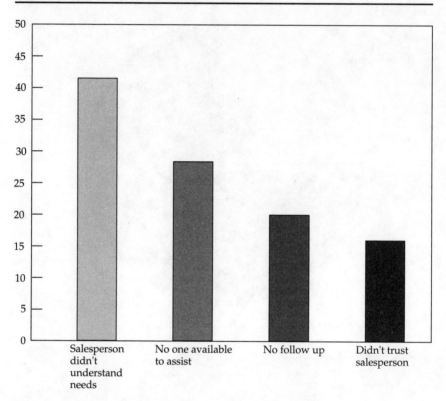

From the Trade Show Bureau, © 1992. Used with permission.

of personnel and time.[4] But, as important, your exhibition will also be a significant investment in your corporate image, and a poorly planned and supported exhibition can tarnish, rather than polish, that image. Professional sales prospecting at a convention and trade is therefore crucial to your success (see Exhibit 14–3).

Exhibit space is often viewed as the only opportunity for convention promotion. However, other avenues are often available for companies that have earned the endorsement of an

EXHIBIT 14–3
Sales Prospecting at the Exhibit

- Wear standard business attire and comfortable shoes.
- Arrive at the exhibit at least 15 minutes early and stay at least 15 minutes late each day.
- Wear your name badge on the right side so that the badge faces their direction when you shake hands.
- Speak slowly and clearly.
- Don't carry on extensive conversations with fellow staff members.
- Don't smoke, eat, or drink, even when invited by a customer.
- Greet people at the edge of the aisle, not back in the booth.
- Never sit down. Appear ready to help.
- Never start a conversation with, "Can I help you?" or with similar questions that can be answered with a simple yes or no.
- Introduce yourself and ask a leading question ("What do you do?" or "Do you have any special purpose for attending the exposition?").
- Use the first minute to qualify the prospect. Does this prospect have the authority to buy your product or service, or to influence the buying decision? Then decide whether or not to proceed with a sales presentation.
- Describe briefly how your product can satisfy the prospect's needs.
- Ask about buying interest within five minutes ("Are you interested in this? Should we meet later back in the office? Do you think what we have fits your needs?").
- If an attendee comes to your exhibit to complain about your product or service, lead them to an area in your booth which is out of hearing range of other prospects. If necessary, take them to the snack bar for a cup of coffee.
- Remain polite and professional. You must control the contact and know when to end it.
- Try to schedule appointments with current customers during the times when the show floor will most likely be less active. Save busy hours for prospecting for new customers.
- Do the paperwork for leads or orders right away. Write clearly.
- Schedule a short daily meeting so that your sales staff at the exhibit can get answers to problems that have surfaced during the course of the event.
- Allow time for your exhibit staff to meet with customers and learn about new developments in your industry by scouting the exposition.
- None of your exhibit staff should work longer than two hours without a break. Allow 15–30 minute breaks to help them recharge batteries and remain alert and friendly.

From *Expositions Work*, 2nd ed., Trade Show Bureau, © 1992. Reprinted with permission.

association, and each one provides unique access to the association's membership:

Special interest sessions. The association may be willing to schedule a special interest session at its convention to introduce the association's program. Such sessions often last an hour or so and give you an opportunity to offer hands-on demonstrations and answer specific questions. Your odds of securing such a session and attracting a crowd increase if you can package your program within a larger topic that is of interest to the membership, rather than simply offering a general sales session. If, for example, you offer an insurance program, you might suggest a session on controlling healthcare costs.

Dawnbuster sessions. An alternative to special interest sessions, held during normal convention hours, are sessions which begin before normal business sessions. These sessions are often held at 7 or 8 AM and offer early risers coffee and an opportunity to learn of new programs. The attendance at early sessions is often surprisingly strong, since the sessions face little competition from other convention events.

Hospitality suites. Companies often find that hosting an open house for association members provides an opportunity to meet the company's leadership on a one-to-one basis. The effectiveness of hospitality suites can often be increased by sending out invitations to members, especially those association members who are already customers, both to thank them for their business and obtain testimonial to the quality of your work or product.

Advertising

Your promotional efforts have laid the groundwork for a successful advertising campaign. The success of the campaign will once again be based on your ability to integrate the advertising channels and endorsement of the association with a message that is customized for the association's membership.

EXHIBIT 14–4
Association Advertising Access

Association Publication	Advertising?	Media Kits?	SRDS?
Magazines	87%	75%	33%
Journals	81	77	41
Newsletters	36	35	n/a
Newspapers	86	75	15

From *Association Publication Procedure*, American Society of Association Executives, © 1991. Used with permission.

Association magazines/newsletters. Gale Research Corporation estimates that there are now more than 12,000 association publications, including some of the largest circulation magazines in the country, such as *Modern Maturity*, published by the American Association of Retired People, with over 32,000,000 members. Studies of association members have found that members rank the association's publications as one of the most important benefits of membership. Unlike general circulation publications, association magazines are targeted to specific member interests and provide one of the few forums for industry-specific information and the exchange of relevant ideas. The respect that members accord these publications can often extend to the advertisers who appear in the publications.[5]

The challenge of marketers is that while the majority of association publications accept advertising, most do not appear on news stands, less than half are listed in Standard Rate and Data Service (SRDS), and only one in six employs a full-time advertising manager.[6] It is for these reasons that some consider association publications one of advertising's best kept secrets.

In addition to advertising, many associations offer merchandising support for advertisers, including: the rental or sale of mailing lists (41 percent); mailing labels (32 percent); reprints (33 percent) and advertising support (21 percent).[7]

To be effective, association advertising must be an ongoing effort to keep your name and the program in front of the membership. All too often, companies limit their advertising

Association Advertising Phrases That Sell

- Buying power
- Buying leverage
- Quality products at quantity
  prices
- Now you have the clout of
  thousands
- You save and support the
  association
- Bottom-line benefits
- Why go it alone?
- Buy with confidence

---

frequency and therefore limit their influence on the buying habits of the membership. Members can only order or ask for your program if they know how to find you—tell them and tell them again.

For companies that have earned the endorsement of the association, the association's publications may offer additional methods to increase member awareness, program recognition, and corporate credibility. At a minimum, endorsed advertisers should promote the name of the association program, not simply the name of their corporation or its products. After all, you have worked hard to earn the association's support—make every effort to promote it. In addition, most associations will permit endorsed vendors to display the association name or logo in their advertisements. Unless advertising includes the program or association's name, members will be unable to distinguish your advertisement from those of any other advertiser, and the clout of the association's endorsement will be wasted.

One of the most effective association advertising techniques is the use of member testimonials. Association members respect the opinions of other association members and view their support as validation of the advertiser's claims. Testimonials of satisfied members can provide insight into how the program assisted members or their businesses. Since the value of testimonials is related to their perceived integrity, testimonials should include, at a minimum, the member's name and location.

Many companies restrict their advertising to the association's magazines or newsletters, overlooking other alternatives. For example, associations often accept advertising in membership catalogs, membership directories, and various other media. In addition, while most associations do not accept advertising in research materials or books, they often do seek corporate support to conduct the research, which is recognized within the completed work. These alternatives often provide advertising and promotional placement that extends for a full year or more, without the competition that accompanies most other advertising.

Sales Efforts

One of the most neglected parts of an association marketing plan is the company's sales force. Whether the sale is made via mail order, sales representatives, or telemarketing, an effective marketing strategy must both inform and motivate.

The sales force. Nothing is more frustrating than an inquiring member who is unable to receive program information because no one is familiar with the program. There are several avenues to increase the awareness, acceptance, and activation of the sales force:

Orientation. Invite the association to speak at a sales meeting and provide an review of the association's membership and the program's development. The association can also detail how the association selected the company and chose its products for endorsement and how it will support the program and its marketing.

Membership awareness. Keep the sales force informed as to the issues facing the association's members. One option is to provide each salesperson with a subscription to the association's magazine and newsletter to enable the sales force to walk in the shoes of the association's members.

Recognition. Recognize those sales people who lead the company in association sales and invite the association to attend an annual sales or awards meeting. The annual event can reinforce both the company's and the association's ongoing commitment to the program. Another option is to conduct an annual sales campaign and award the winners with attendance at the association's convention, which are usually held at resort locales.

Leads. Provide your sales force with a list of members and a list of sales and promotional events within their territories. After all, if your promotional and advertising efforts are successful, qualified leads are the ultimate sales force motivator.

Bart Schramm, Xerox's U.S. customer operations manager, sums it up, "Association programs enable the sales force to take the chill off of the cold call. After all, a quality membership list of an association that has endorsed our products is a sales person's dream come true."

Telemarketing. One of the most effective and efficient tools in association marketing is telemarketing; unfortunately, it is often resisted by associations. Associations often think of telemarketing as "boiler room" operations, operated by high pressure salespeople. The worst fear of association executives is that members will be hounded by commission-driven marketers and that the association's goodwill will be placed in jeopardy. To penetrate the association's preconceptions, companies must increase their comfort level regarding the purpose and value of program telemarketing:

Center visits. Invite the association to tour the telemarketing operations and visit with people who will be conducting and supervising membership calls. The visit could include a presentation by the association's leadership or staff to ensure that the telemarketing staff are familiar with the association and have an opportunity to ask questions.

Purpose of call. Telemarketing can be used to introduce a program, respond to an initial inquiry, close a sale, or follow up a sale. By clarifying the purposes of the program's telemarketing, the association's resistance may be reduced or eliminated.

Script approval. Associations should be provided a copy of telemarketing scripts and an opportunity for input. This review will ensure that standard scripts are customized for the association's membership and properly reflect the image of the association.

Sell your "legs." Most associations lack marketing "legs"; telemarketing can provide a powerful tool for the association to reach its membership and sell the benefits of both the program and the association itself. The more your calls sell the association, the higher your odds of success.

Association information. Successful telemarketing is often characterized by a sales force that is familiar with the association and can talk its language. Providing your telemarketing staff with the association's magazine and newsletters permits them to talk the association's language and relate the product or service to member concerns.

Follow-up. Keep the association informed as to results of the telemarketing, especially as it compares to other marketing efforts. Marketing results will help the association recognize the value of telemarketing and ensure its continued use.

Support

Regardless of the promotional, advertising, and sales efforts that you employ, your long-term success will be judged by your ongoing support of the program. Members rely on the programs of the association because they are both reliable and competitive. Often a corporation's support of a program will be gauged by the extent to which it recognizes the unique needs of the association's membership through its marketing, sales, and promotional efforts, as well as by the performance of the company's products. After all, while some products or programs offered through an association are truly unique, most are available outside of the association. Therefore, the goal is to differentiate the program from other options available.

Support of the program can be exhibited to the members of the association both during and after the sale. Support includes all commitments to ensure the program's relevancy and quality and customer satisfaction:

Service after the sale. This includes the continued support of the product or service after the sale has been closed, including customer service and warranty support. These are vital parts of a marketing plan and should be highlighted within marketing materials to increase the buying confidence of members.

"Satisfaction guaranteed." Often, to distinguish association programs, corporations offer members a satisfaction guarantee. The commitment usually provides that if the member is dissatisfied, the product will be either repaired or replaced or monies refunded. This provision can be especially effective if it is unique to the association's program.

Member hotline. Some corporations support their association programs with an 800 number that is exclusive to their association programs. Such hotlines permit the corporation to centrally track association inquiries and ensure that operators are familiar with the association program and its members.

Product development. No program should be allowed to stagnate—it should respond to the changing needs of the association's membership by the addition of needed products or services and the replacement of others that are no longer relevant. The association provides unique access and the opportunity to develop products and services in response to member requests. Once the corporation is an endorsed vendor, most subsequent approvals are expedited.

Association surveys are an effective vehicle for determining membership needs and promoting the benefits of the existing program. Members want to provide their association with input; it is not unusual for association surveys to have response rates of 30 to 40 percent. While the survey results provide valuable guidance, those members who respond often represent a potent target market.

Quality assurance. Members and the association want to be ensured that the products and services being offered are fulfilling their expectations and the vendor's promises. By conducting quality-assurance surveys, both the commitment and confidence of the association and the members will be increased. The surveys are also an excellent means to pinpoint additional needs and gauge the adequacy of your marketing, sales, and support. Remember that good quality-assurance survey results should be promoted actively in your advertising, direct mail, press releases, and association magazine articles.

Associations and their members are seeking assurance that they will not be left high and dry. The ongoing support of corporate partners exhibits both their commitment and confidence in the program, while increasing the buying confidence of the members.

THE MARKETING PLAN

While the association and the corporation have significant resources that can be employed to leverage association marketing, none of them will be adequately tapped without planning. Each component of the marketing plan requires lead time, the cooperation of other parties, coordination with other plan elements, and budget review.

A marketing plan should establish the implementation schedule and set the expectations for each party. The plan should enable both parties to anticipate events and evaluate ongoing and unexpected opportunities. At a minimum, a marketing plan should include:

- A list of the resources to be utilized. The list should detail specific promotional, advertising, sales, and support elements that will be implemented. The elements should be listed, where possible, in the order that they are to be implemented to ensure that lead times are considered and elements coordinated.
- Who is responsible for each element of the plan. For each element of the plan, an individual should be identified who will be responsible for development, coordination, and

approval. This step can save endless frustration and avoid the "I thought you were responsible" shuffle. While the association and corporate program managers may be the liaisons, it's likely that other individuals within the association and the corporation are responsible for creative development or advertising placement.

• When the element is due. Due dates need to be determined after a review of required lead times for each of the elements, such as magazine articles, advertising, and direct mail. The due date should permit each party time for development, review, approval, and implementation.

• Follow-up required. Once an element has been delivered, it may require approval, implementation, or distribution coordinated by the other party. Many times this final step proves to be the stumbling block, as each party awaits the necessary approval of the other party; therefore, agree upon a turn-around time and encourage the use of fax and overnight mail.

MONITORING

The marketing plan should be reviewed quarterly to evaluate its effectiveness, evaluate new resources, and adjust to reflect changing market conditions and member needs. One option is to review the plan in conjunction with the payment of the royalties or the reporting of program marketing results. Since most agreements require that royalties and sales be reported or paid on a quarterly or semi-annual basis, their presentation provides an excellent opportunity to review the program and the adequacy of its marketing.

Remember that a successful marketing plan is one that integrates both the provider and the association. By working toward mutual goals, individual goals will be achieved—the association will generate nondues income and provide services that attract and retain members, and the partner will retain and increase market share.

EXHIBIT 14–5
Association Marketing Plan Components (PASS)

Element	Responsible Party	Due Date	Follow-up Required	Due Date	Implementation Required
Promotion					
Offer's Design					
Press releases					
Corporate					
Association					
Association publications					
Articles					
Columns					
Direct mail campaign					
Trade show					
Exposition					
Special interest sessions					
"Dawnbusters"					
Hospitality suite					
Sponsorships					
Advertising					
Association advertisements					
Magazine					
Newsletter					
Journal					
Other publications					
Sales efforts					
Sales orientation					
Lead distribution					
Telemarketing					
Recognition					
Support					
Member "hotline"					
Quality surveys					

MARKETING—KEYS TO SUCCESS

1. Leverage the resources of both parties. While your corporation has product and marketing expertise, the association has exclusive communication channels that can both motivate and market. You have harnessed the endorsement of the association—take advantage of it.

2. Recognize that a long-term commitment is needed. Success will not come overnight, nor in the first 100 days. The association must be viewed as a pivotal strategy for your future growth.

3. Prepare a written marketing plan. In conjunction with the association, prepare a marketing plan that is a living document, subject to change based on results and market conditions. The plan needs to include promotion, advertising, sales, and support—the PASS system.

4. Hold someone responsible. The implementation of the marketing plan will encompass many divisions of your operation. For each element of the program, assign responsibility and then hold your program manager responsible for its monitoring.

5. Sell your sales force. Your sales force are the eyes, ears and image of your company—if they are not sold on the benefits of the partnership, sales will suffer. Involve the association during the orientation and the sales force in the marketing plan.

6. Exhibit your endorsement. Incorporate the association's endorsement in all your promotional, advertising, and sales activities. While running your standard industry advertisements may save time in the short term, ignoring the association's name and endorsement will cost you in the long term.

7. Target, do not broadcast. The association endorsement provides you the ability to match your message to the market. As you develop advertising and direct mail, remember the common traits of the membership, then customize.

8. Explore alternative strategies. When developing your marketing plan, remember that many options exist that are unique to associations. These alternative approaches often provide exclusive access to the membership, complement other sales and promotional efforts, and enhance your results.

9. Monitor the plan. In conjunction with the royalty or sales reports, review the program's results and modify the marketing

plan. After all, you want increased sales and the association wants to see strong participation and rising royalties.

10. The bottom line: When members think of the association, they should think of you.

NOTES

1. Trade Show Bureau, *10*10*10 Years of Trade Show Bureau Reports in Ten Minutes* (Trade Show Bureau, 1991), p. 3.
2. Edward Chapman, Jr. (ed.), *Expositions Work* (Trade Show Bureau, 1992), p. 28.
3. Trade Show Bureau, p. 13.
4. Chapman, p. 13.
5. Ron Bognore, "Professional and Trade Associations: Direct Connections to Your Markets," *Business Marketing* (September 1992), p. 4.
6. American Society of Association Executives, *Association Publication Procedures* (ASAE, 1991), p. 4.
7. Ibid.

Chapter Fifteen

Managing the Relationship

We have discussed the association market, its motivations, opportunities, prospecting, decision making, and marketing. It is obvious that although our rewards will not come overnight, the potential is worth the effort. Whichever our approach to tap the association market, whether by marketing through the association or in partnership with the association, the relationship will take work. Maintaining an effective working relationship is equally as important as the program development.[1]

PROFIT-NONPROFIT CULTURE GAP

One of the many challenges of the association market is bridging the profit-nonprofit cultural gap. The cultural differences between the association and its corporate suitor influence their ongoing relationship, and the recognition of the differences provides the key to a successful relationship.

One of the first cultural confrontations experienced by corporations is the decision-making process of associations. While corporations usually have delineated organizational charts, with each position having determined decision-making capability, associations rely heavily on their volunteer members for advice and often for the final decision. While the consensus decision-making process ensures board input, infrequent meetings and committee turnover can delay key decisions. The association's lack of a single decision maker can also affect corporate time schedules, as the association's considerations stretch past corporate annual planning and budget processes.

While the association's decision-making process can be cumbersome, it can also work to your benefit if you design programs that meet the needs of the membership. For, if members view the program as critical or as one which helps their businesses or profession, approval and implementation can often be accelerated. In addition, once a corporation sells its commitment to the association and its members, the long decision-making process can often forestall the entry, or the association's future consideration of, a competitor.

In addition, according to Mark French of French & Associates, "While the decision-making process may seem daunting, the investment of time can pay significant dividends. For rather than negotiating with one customer at a time, the association enables corporations to negotiate thousands of relationships at once."

Corporations can also be frustrated by the frequent lack of full-time association staff to develop and implement services. Many associations are, in fact, small businesses, and therefore many employees wear many hats. Recognizing this shortcoming in some associations, corporations should propose programs that are turnkey and offer the association the ability to implement without new staff or other significant expenditures. By leveraging the communication channels of the association with the product and marketing expertise of the corporation partner, the association can appear, in the eyes of its members, larger than it is, while still providing its corporate partner the additional clout and goodwill needed to gain market share.

Corporations are also often surprised by the level of association satisfaction with programs that they view as marginal, and by association disappointment with programs that corporations view as successful. Companies often view results from a financial point of view, either by income or market share, while associations usually take a longer view and value nonfinancial factors such as member satisfaction and the program's affect on membership retention and recruitment. By establishing mutual program goals and marketing expectations, the parties can agree upon a set of standards on which to judge the program's success.

In addition, when association partnerships are established, partners often ignore the impact of combining the communication systems of two organizations, one profit and one nonprofit, and thus the communication problems of both bureaucratic structures are exacerbated.[2] Often good programs don't fail because they fail to perform, but because the organizations fail to communicate; small problems become large problems and rumors are accepted as fact.

RELATIONSHIP–KEYS TO SUCCESS

Recognizing these cultural differences provide the basis for the keys to the management of an association partnership:

Communication. The bottom line of association communication can be summed up in two words—"no surprises." In association partnerships, both you and the association's good name are on the line and open communication will ensure that both are protected. Issues that affect a corporation can quickly affect its products, program support, and image. An association that is prepared for membership inquiries can often allay member concerns and increase their buying confidence.

We all want to broadcast our successes and hide our failures. But often, if we achieve our goal, our success will be taken for granted and our failures will be dismissed as incidental. One of the surest signs of a bad relationship is a lack of complaints, for no one is that satisfied over a extended period.[3] After all, the association's largest asset is its goodwill, and each program is an extension of that goodwill. By establishing communication systems that are open and informal, issues can be addressed and problems quickly resolved. If the association is informed and involved, it can be an advocate, not simply a sponsor.

Relationships also require an ongoing effort to understand one another. When an industry or occupation is facing problems, its association will mirror those problems. Take the time to communicate with the association and understand its challenges, for each challenge represents opportunities to assist and grow with the association and its members. When times get tough, associations remember those who helped.

Program review. The book, *Enterprise in the Nonprofit Sector*, by James C. Crimmins and Mary Keil, which surveyed the results of various nonprofit partnerships, concludes that "today's success can easily become tomorrow's failure. Enterprise requires perseverance and a dedication to rethinking and reworking each twist in the chain of event."⁴ One of the hallmarks of a successful partnership is the commitment to monitor the program's performance.

While the long decision-making process of the association ensures member input, it can also delay implementation and cause programs that were believed to meet member needs to become outdated. The partnership, through a concerted process of member review and quality assurance surveys, can ensure that the program continues to meet member needs and remains a valued part of their membership.

Marketing analysis. Both you and the association have capabilities and expertise that can be leveraged to ensure efficient and effective marketing. The association has exclusive member communication channels, and you have product, sales, marketing, and advertising resources. Your success will depend on your ability to integrate your promotion, sales, advertising, and support.

Regardless of your efforts, according to the book, *Something Ventured, Something Gained,* by Laura Landy, which details the business development process of nonprofit organizations, "Marketing will take more time and more money than expected; sales will develop more slowly than expected, and cash will be received more slowly than expected."⁵ Through the constant review and evaluation of marketing efforts, the parties are able to target membership segments, focus efforts on geographic areas, and add products to ensure that the program achieves the partnership's marketing and revenue goals.

Common vision. Establish with the association common goals and objectives for the program. Through the building of a common vision, you and the association will establish a basis on which to judge the program, its shortcomings, and, more importantly, agree to changes to ensure its success. The establishment of a common vision may also encompass the sharing of your budget or sales goals and the association's sharing of its revenue or nondues income goals for the program.

Through the sharing of goals, one sales and one nondues, both parties have a vested interest in working to achieve them. Without common goals, a company may be disappointed with program sales, while the association may be satisfied with membership response. Therefore, while the company may push for additional marketing, the association may be satisfied with existing efforts.

Responsibility. Programs and marketing plans must be implemented and supported by both parties, each of whom contributes resources and expertise. To succeed, each party must select an individual who will be held accountable for the implementation and marketing of the program. While the respective program managers will draw on the expertise and talents of others in their respective organizations, it is critical that each party appoint one central point of contact and therefore avoid the "I-thought-you-were-going-to-do-it" syndrome.

Talk the language. As you develop marketing materials and orient your sales force, talk the language of the association. Keep your sales force up to date through orientations with the association and receipt of the association's magazine or newsletter. After all, the sales force is your association goodwill ambassador.

Honor your staff. For each new service there is a staff person who is held responsible and accountable. These staffers field member inquiries, answer questions, respond to complaints, report to the association's leadership, and, more importantly, are the corporate partner's umbilical cord. If the staff is kept in the dark, they, and ultimately your program, are vulnerable. The worst answer that an association can give to an inquiring member is "I don't know."

Independent but dependent. Despite the partnership, the corporation and the association will remain independent operations. While each organization will continue to service its customers or members, remember that your success depends on the success of the association and the prosperity of the industry or profession that it represents.

THE BOTTOM LINE

The success of your program depends on the success and prosperity of the association's membership. A successful program will help the association achieve its goal of attracting and retaining members and building nondues income, will assist members' profitability or product access, and will help build sales and market share for the corporate partner—a win-win-win.

NOTES

1. Mirlam Meister, "Marketing Sponsored Products and Services," *Marketing the Nonprofit Association* (GWSAE Foundation, 1992), p. 183.
2. *Study of Cause-related Marketing*, (Independent Sector, 1988), p. 31.
3. Theodore Levitt, *The Marketing Imagination* (The Free Press, 1986), p. 119.
4. James C. Crimmins and Mary Keil, *Enterprise in the Nonprofit Sector* (Partners for Livable Places, 1983), p. 122.
5. Laura Landy, *Something Ventured, Something Gained* (ACA Books, 1989), p. 134.

Chapter Sixteen

The Future of Association Partnerships

The future of association partnerships depends on satisfying the needs of the corporate partner and the association. For the partnership to be viable it must enable both parties to achieve strategic goals in an efficient and effective manner. The corporate partner is seeking the ability to target market by leveraging the association's name and goodwill, and associations are seeking to attract and retain members while building a reliable source of nondues income. The continued viability and expansion of association marketing will be determined by the changing needs of the corporate partner, the continued growth of existing associations, and the formation of new associations.

THE CORPORATE PARTNER

In light of increasing bottom line pressure, both domestically and internationally, it seems certain that American businesses will continue their efficiency quest. While many companies have responded by downsizing, more popularly called "rightsizing," eliminating divisions and reducing middle management and production capacity, other companies have used the hard times to strengthen their position through acquisitions, by recruiting more qualified personnel, and by increasing operational efficiency.

The "how to do more with less" business philosophy will certainly affect traditional sales and marketing methods. Companies will continue to examine their sales costs, often reducing them through the elimination of regional or local support and through a corresponding dependence on centralized operations; through the utilization of catalog and telemarketing sales to supplement or complement current one-on-one sales efforts; and, where appropriate, through an increased reliance on bulk sales through clubs and warehouses.

While many of the changes in sales and marketing will be bottom-line driven, others will be fostered by the public's growing acceptance of alternative delivery systems. For the public is becoming increasingly comfortable with doing business, not just across the street but across the country, via telephone or the mail. The public has found, all too often, that such long-distance shopping, rather then diminishing customer support, actually enhances it, that advice is frequently more available and accurate, and, bottom line, that their costs are lower and delivery often faster.

The corporation's need to increase sales efficiency, through target marketing and exploring centralized support systems, bodes well for the continued usage of association partnerships. For associations enable corporations to target market and increase the effectiveness and efficiency of their sales and marketing efforts. While other conduits provide the opportunity to establish target markets, associations represent a market, not simply of people or businesses that share common buying habits, but who are often motivated by the actions of their peers and their belief in the association.

The future of association partnerships, will also depend on the growth and needs of existing associations and the formation of new associations.

ASSOCIATION GROWTH

Like their corporate suitors, associations will continue to face bottom-line challenges, driven by the ups and downs of membership dues and the increasing demands of their members. While the growth of nondues revenue has reduced the dependence on dues, dues continue to be the single largest source of association income. While nondues income now accounts for more than 50 percent of association income, only 5 percent of total association income is generated from royalty income or the sale of products, according to the *Operating Ratio Report* of the ASAE.[1]

The emergence of association services has provided associations with a powerful membership magnet that has both attracted and retained members. While the services of the association have provided added value to membership, they often increase member expectations and fuel the development of additional services and programs to enable the association to answer the membership question: "What have you done for me lately?"

As members demand the development and support of an increasing array of services and programs, the association will change to support those needs.

Staff-driven. According to James Dunlop, author of *Leading the Association*, "The trend to become more staff-driven, seen clearly during the past ten years, will continue as associations grow and become more complex in organization and operations and more professional in their staffing."[2] While the movement toward staff-driven associations can risk the diminishment of member input, it can add to the expertise of associations and their ability to evaluate, implement, market, and support programs.

While the increased influence of association staffing is often viewed as simply a by-product of association entrepreneurship, it is also being driven by what some have called "a new breed of member."[3] These members, often unlike the historical members of associations, are not as interested in being involved in the association's leadership or influencing the association's direction. These new members, often the managers of business rather than the owners of businesses, are frequently less concerned about the association's social functions and more concerned with issues that will affect their bottom line, such as government affairs, taxation, and regulation. Unfortunately, this new breed often have less time to be involved in the day-to-day affairs of the association, and therefore associations often take on additional staff to assume responsibilities once performed by volunteers.[4]

Staff will become more specialized. As associations become more complex, association staffing will become more specialized. While the staffing of many associations will continue to be characterized by few people wearing many hats, many others will add specialized professionals to support the bottom-line demands of their membership. The first areas to experience staff specialization are those that affect the majority of members and that can best display the association's commitment, such as educational programs, governmental affairs, regulatory support, and association services.

One of the dilemmas faced by corporations, for example, is identifying the staffer within the association responsible for the development of services and programs. In the past this role was often viewed simply as a part-time task within a full-time job, such as membership recruitment, marketing, or administration. As associations have added services, they have also begun to add specialized staff to manage their implementation and support. According to the *U.S. News and World Report*, "member services director" was listed as the "Hot Professional Track in the Non-profit Sector" (see Exhibit 16–1). According to the article, "As membership has neared the saturation level, competing for new recruits and keeping the ranks happy have made the member services director a very important person."[5]

Associations more businesslike. In the book, *Leading the Association*, author James Dunlop states that "continued development of nondues income sources, coupled with increased staff specialization and professionalism, will cause associations to function in a more businesslike manner. There will be more internal controls over costs, more detailed reporting of operations to the board, more emphasis on efficiency to conserve revenue, and greater attention to the bottom line."[6] It is not a coincidence that as associations begin to operate more like businesses, they face the same challenge as their corporate suitors: how to do more with less.

Like their corporate partners, association service decisions will also become more focused and market-based. Associations will base new services on surveys and member research and evaluate their implementation based on the relationship between the potential revenue and the investment required of the association, whether capital or staff.

EXHIBIT 16–1
1993 Career Guide–Hot Professional Track: Nonprofit

Member Services Director

Nearly 100,000 professional and trade associations exist in the United States, from the American Automobile Association to the American Association of Zoo Keepers. That's about 40 percent more than a decade ago; 7 out of 10 Americans belong to at least one such group. As membership has neared the saturation level, competing for new recruits and keeping the ranks happy have made the member services director a very important person. The work might entail arranging a health-benefits program, planning educational seminars and putting out publications. Member services staff might help figure out ways to educate the public about issues of concern to the association and perhaps organize activist members into a political lobby.

Average Salary
Entry: $18,000–$25,000
Midlevel: $32,000–$38,000
Top: $45,000–$60,000
Pros and Cons. Salaries are generally lower than in the corporate world, though the do-good aspect of working for a nonprofit is reward enough for many. Freedom from bottom-line worries allows more risk taking. Staffs can be small, which means a hefty workload.
Training. A liberal arts degree with course work in business administration is a good start. An advanced degree in human resources is valuable, as is experience.
Best Places. Cities like Washington and New York where associations are headquartered.
Other Hot Tracks. Fund-raising/planned-giving manager.

U.S. News & World Report, Copyright, October 26, 1992.

Greater risk taking. As associations find success in the offering of products and services, their willingness to take risks will likely increase. Associations quickly become aware that the greater the risk, the greater the reward, and each successful service builds the association's confidence in ventures which not only place the association's name or goodwill at risk, but often its capital as well.

Associations have often found that their entrepreneurship is contagious, and that when members recognize that the association can actually help in solving problems, rather than simply observe or interpret changes, services quickly become a team sport. It is not unusual, therefore, to find associations that once simply endorsed services, later forming service corporations or joint ventures to manufacture, promote, distribute, or deliver needed member services. Certainly, as the association risk-taking comfort increases, the opportunities for association partnerships expand.

While associations will continue to grow to meet their members' needs, other associations will be formed to meet underserved needs. Each new association will represent new target markets and new opportunities for association partnerships.

NEW ASSOCIATIONS

With more than 100,000 associations now in existence at the national, state, and local levels, many assume that their years of growth are behind them. Yet, experts predict that 1,000 new organizations will be formed annually. Associations are forming today to address new causes, represent new industries or professions, and to achieve common goals members could not achieve on an individual basis.

In 1991, spawned by new restrictions on the deductibility of home interest and the decline in the percentage of Americans who owned homes, the United Homeowners Association was formed to represent the interests of America's 65 million homeowners, who represent over $2 trillion in purchasing power. The main purpose of the group is to serve as the lobbying arm on behalf of the homeowners to protect the tax-favored treatment of home ownership.

For $12 a year, the association provides its 22,000 members with a bimonthly newsletter, a toll-free number to answer consumer questions about real estate, and discounts on home-related services. While the upstart association has a staff of only four, the association works in conjunction with other associations with similar interests, such as realtors, insurance companies, and bankers, to achieve common goals. To ensure that the research and information about home ownership is maintained and disseminated, the association has also founded a foundation that seeks the funding support of corporations and other interested parties.

While Americans over the age of 50 are represented by the 34 million-member American Association of Retired Persons, many of the country's 80 million baby boomers (those born between 1943–1964) have also been looking for an advocate. In 1989, the American Association of Boomers (AAB) was founded in Dallas, Texas. The association's mission is to promote "positive change," press for the long-term financial viability of the Social Security system, and promote voter registration among baby boomers.

The American Association of Boomers charges a modest $10 annual fee and provides members a bimonthly publication, access to group discounts, and a forum for legislative advocacy. Since its inception, AAB has attracted over 25,000 members and spawned the establishment of over 50 chapters in 14 states.

In order to advocate responsible nonsmoking legislation against the financial resources of the tobacco industry, the National Association of Nonsmokers was begun in 1990. The association was founded to represent nonsmokers, educate children about the relationship between smoking and health, and help members recognize their rights as nonsmokers. For annual dues of only $10 per year, members receive benefits and services including hotel discounts and travel services.

While leisure airfares may have declined, business travelers, who usually lack flexibility, often pay full freight and essentially subsidize other passengers. In 1992, the Commercial Travelers Association was formed to represent the needs of business travelers, who often lack the individual clout to negotiate airline and hotel discounts. The association's goal is to recruit 5 million members in the next 10 years.

The association, for an annual membership fee of $5, provides members with a newsletter and is developing member services that include a credit card, discounts on tires, gasoline, and car rental, and, of course, discounts on motel, hotel, and airline fares.

While many associations are formed to represent broad-based interests, others are established to address more limited, perhaps even seasonal, needs. One group, for example, has been formed to promote keeping the cost of gifts in check. The group, SCROOGE, the Society to Curtail Ridiculous, Outrageous, and

Ostentatious Gift Exchange, has grown to 1,300 members in the United States, Canada, and England. SCROOGE urges people to not to use credit cards and to limit their Christmas gifts to no more that 0.5 percent of their annual incomes.

Regardless of the cause, desire, or unfilled need, associations will continue to be formed and their members will continue to demand an ever-growing menu of services. Several lifestyle and workplace trends will likely spur the establishment of an increasing array of associations:

• Healthcare. One of the most difficult issues facing the government and the nation's businesses is the provision of healthcare. With business healthcare cost rising by 16 percent annually through the 1980s and the increased national attention being received by the nation's uninsured, it seems inevitable that associations will be formed to advocate healthcare approaches and ensure that legislative initiatives do not negatively affect their members' businesses or professions.

• Daycare. The increased utilization by families of daycare services for both infants and the elderly will increase the national focus on the need for quality daycare and the establishment and monitoring of standards to ensure its delivery. Associations will likely be established to focus on daycare centers, home-based daycare operators, and related healthcare issues.

• Home businesses. With the advent of personal computers and lower communications costs, more professionals are able to operate branch offices or stand-alone businesses from their homes. These professionals will have different needs and likely require new associations to represent their interests.

• "Retired" workers. In this age of downsizing, many corporations have offered workers early retirement options. These workers, unlike their "gold watch" counterparts, have up to 20 years for alternative or second careers. This new work force will likely find representation in some existing groups, but many other associations will likely be formed to meet their needs and ensure the integrity of their promised retirement benefits.

• Work force diversity. According to the U.S. Department of Labor, 80 percent of all job entrants between the years 1990 and 2000 will be minorities, immigrants, or women. As minorities and women become more dominant in the workplace, they will likely seek out associations that represent their professions and are sensitive to their cultural needs. This increased work force diversity will spawn associations to meet the specific needs of minority professionals and businesses. While some of these associations will certainly be affiliates of existing associations, others will represent new challenges to their association counterparts.

• International emphasis. As more companies seek to expand overseas, the need to understand the cultures and customs of other countries will expand rapidly. As the international flavor of business increases, new or existing associations will be asked to take more active roles in standardizing products and components to facilitate member bidding and export.

• Increased role of the private sector to replace or supplement historically governmental roles. As both federal and state governments face budget constraints, individuals and businesses will look to associations to provide assistance that they are unable to provide on an individual basis. In 1923, Secretary of Commerce Herbert Hoover observed, "With wisdom and devotion, their [associations'] voluntary forces can accomplish more for our country than any spread of the hand of government."[7]

• Rising regulatory burdens. As the Congress and government agencies increase the array of regulations that businesses and professionals face, associations will increasingly influence the regulation debate and drafting, interpret those that are enacted, and assist members to comply.

• New technologies. Every new technology spawns new occupations and specialties that will require representation and continuing education and information to meet their needs. While many existing associations will change to meet those needs, other associations will also be formed to represent the needs of the specialized group.

• Influence. Americans, whether individuals or businesses, are increasingly joining groups that advocate their opinions, beliefs, professions, or occupations and are quickly learning the benefits of working together to accomplish change. Associations provide the ultimate system of checks and balances;

for every law or regulation proposed, there is likely an association that represents its proponents and one that represents its opponents.

THE BOTTOM LINE

The potential of association partnerships depends on the need of corporations to target market with the strong "seal of approval" of associations and the need of new and existing associations to meet their members' needs. As both corporations and associations seek to accomplish more with less, it seems certain that association partnerships will flourish.

NOTES

1. American Society of Association Executives, *Association Operating Ratio Report* (ASAE, 1989), p. 1.
2. James Dunlop, *Leading the Association* (ASAE, 1989), p. 139.
3. Ibid., p. 118.
4. Ibid., p. 119.
5. "Hot Tracks in 20 Professions," *U.S. News and World Report* (October 26, 1992), p. 108.
6. Dunlop, p. 141.
7. *Association Fact Book*, p. 14.

CONCLUSION

Companies spend billions of dollars attempting to establish target markets in order to improve the efficiency and effectiveness of their marketing. Such targeting focuses marketing, promotional, and advertising resources on prospects who share purchasing habits, occupations, professions, beliefs, or lifestyles. Each association is in fact a target market composed of members that share not only a common bond but also a respect for the association and the services it provides.

Harnessing the leverage of associations with the product and marketing expertise of corporate partners enables both parties to accomplish vital goals. The corporation gains unparalleled access to its target markets, while the association gains an enhanced ability to attract and retain members by providing services that meet member needs.

All too often, companies simply view associations as business prospects and ignore the market that lies beneath—the association's members. For while it is estimated that over 100,000 associations now exist at the national, state, and local levels, those associations represent an estimated 500 million Americans.

Glossary of Association Terms (talk the language)

As you develop an association program, wear the association's hat and use the association's lingo.

associate membership Corporate association membership available to suppliers to a profession or industry. While associate membership conveys certain privileges, it usually does not imply the association's endorsement of the member or its programs.

chapter An association that has a formal relationship with a parent or umbrella organization and has jurisdiction over a geographic area rather than an area of special interest.

council A group, organization, or association that has jurisdiction over an area of interest, rather than a geographic area (see also *sections*).

CAE A professional designation, "Certified Association Executive," bestowed by the American Society of Association Executives to association executives who have completed specified coursework.

endorsement/sponsorships The support of selected products and services by associations.

executive vice president Most often refers to the chief of staff of the association, rather than the volunteer leader.

foundations Nonprofit entities often established by associations to support the purposes and goals of the association and provide the association with an additional source of nondues income for activities such as education, research, training, and scholarships.

members Corporations work with customers and refer to noncustomers as prospects. Associations, on the other hand, work with members and refer to prospective members as nonmembers. The lifeblood of any association is membership; a well-designed association program provides the association a vehicle to retain and attract members.

member-driven Most associations refer to their program evaluation and decision-making process as member-driven. Since the members are the ultimate users of the proposed services, it is only logical that they be the driving force in its development.

nondues income Associations call any income other than membership dues nondues income. Associations develop nondues income to diversify their financial base and reduce the association's vulnerability to the volatility of membership dues, allowing members to pay as they go, rather than requiring all members to pay for services, whether they are used or not through dues. Nondues income encompasses services and products but also includes educational programs, convention registration, exposition, and investment income.

president Most often refers to the volunteer head of the association, rather than the chief of staff.

royalties Income received by an association for the use of its name and logo.

sections (also referred to as "special interest sections") A group or organization (not an association) that operates with a limited amount of autonomy and has jurisdiction over an area of professional or business interest. Sections often represent specialists or interests within an association.

service corporations For-profit subsidiaries established by associations to manage and market programs. Service corporations also permit associations to add product or management expertise.

Appendix B

The Largest Associations by Membership Size

I. Trade Associations with 25,000 or More Members*

The Institute of Electrical & Electronic Engineers	320,000
United States Chamber of Commerce	200,000
Distributive Education Clubs of America	200,000
National Association of Home Builders	158,000
Robert Morris Association	145,000
Uniform Code Council	100,500
Voluntary Protection Program Participants Association	75,000
American Advertising Federation	54,000
Wheat Ridge Ministries	52,000
National Association of Wholesaler Distributors	40,000
National Association of Credit Management	36,000
National Apartment Association	35,000
Independent Insurance Agents of America	32,000
Association of Governing Boards of Universities and Colleges	31,000
American Defense Preparedness Association	29,000
National Council for the Social Studies	26,000
Florists Transworld Delivery Association	25,000
National Restaurant Association	25,000
International Council of Shopping Centers	25,000

II. Individual Associations with over 3,000,000 Members*

American Automobile Association	33,300,000
American Association of Retired Persons	32,500,000
Young Mens Christian Association	12,800,000
National Right to Life Committee	12,000,000
National Parents Teachers Association	6,800,000
Boy Scouts of America	5,400,000
Evangelical Lutheran Church in America	5,200,000
National Committee to Preserve Social Security and Medicare	5,000,000
HCA Association	5,000,000
Holy Childhood Association	4,500,000
National Council of Senior Citizens	4,000,000
Womens International Bowling Congress	3,700,000
Office of the General Assembly Presbyterian Church	3,500,000
American Farm Bureau Federation	3,400,000
American Heart Association	3,200,000
Girl Scouts of the USA	3,200,000
American Legion	3,100,000
American Bowling Congress	3,100,000
National Rifle Association of America	3,000,000

*Lists include associations that are members of the American Society of Association Executives. Lists reprinted with the permission of the ASAE.

Associations by Budget Size

The following are 25 trade and individual associations with reported budgets in excess of $10 million annually and are members of the American Society of Association Executives:

Trade Associations

Air Transport Association of America
Alliance of American Insurers
American Arbitration Association
American Bankers Association
American College Testing Program
American Council of Life Insurance
American Council on Education
American Electronics Association
American Forest & Paper Association, Inc.
American Hotel & Motel Association
American Iron & Steel Institute
American Management Systems
American Plywood Association
American Trucking Association Federation
Association for Manufacturing Technology
Association of Medical Colleges
Association of American Railroads
Audit Bureau of Circulations
Catholic Heath Association
Chemical Manufactures Association
Council of State Governments
Direct Marketing Association
Edison Electric Association
Electric Power Research Institute

Individual Associations

ASM International
African American Institute
Air Force Association
Aircraft Owners and Pilots Association
Alcoholics Anonymous
Alzheimers Association
American Academy of Orthopaedic Surgeons
American Academy of Family Physicians
American Academy of Ophthalmology
American Academy of Pediatrics
American Association for the Advancement of Science
American Association of Oral and Maxillofacial Surgeons
American Association of Retired Persons
American Bar Association
American Board of Internal Medicine
American Board of Podiatric Surgery
American Bowling Congress
American Cancer Society
American Chemical Society
American College of Cardiology
American College of Emergency Physicians
American College of Healthcare Executives
American College of Physicians
American College of Radiology
American College of Surgeons

Lists reprinted with the permission of the American Society of Association Executives.

Appendix D

Association Magazines

The following publications are representative of the over 12,000 association magazines that are published. The following publications have circulations over 50,000 and are members of the Society of National Association Publications (SNAP). SNAP serves the needs of association and society publications and their staffs.

AABB Technical Manual
American Association of Blood Banks
60,000 circulation
(703) 247–0533

AARP Highlights
American Association of Retired People
200,000 circulation
(202) 434–3407

AAUW Outlook
American Association of University Women
130,000 circulation
(202) 785–7700

ABA Journal
American Bar Association
450,000 circulation
(312) 988–5996

AOPA
Aircraft Owners and Pilots Association
300,000 circulation
(301) 695–2350

ASCD Update
Association for Supervision & Curriculum Development
200,000 circulation
(703) 549–9110

ASHRAE Journal
American Society of Heating, Refrigerating, and Air Conditioning
Engineers
60,000 circulation
(404) 636–8400

Advanced Materials and Process
ASM International
53,000 circulation
(216) 338–5151

American Scientist
The Scientific Research Society
114,000 circulation
(919) 549–0097

Arthritis Today
Arthritis Foundation
500,000 circulation
(404) 872–7100

Balls and Strikes
Amateur Softball Association
300,000 circulation
(405) 424–5266

Barrister
American Bar Association Press
165,000 circulation
(312) 988–6045

Do-It-Yourself Retailing
National Retail Hardware Association
70,000 circulation
(317) 297–1190

Engineering Dimensions
Association of Professional Engineers of Ontario
59,500 circulation
(416) 961–1100

Engineering Times
National Society of Professional Engineers
80,000 circulation
(703) 684–2875

Focus on Critical Care
American Association of Critical Care Nurses
70,000 circulation
(714) 362–2050

Greenpeace Magazine
Greenpeace
1.5 million circulation
(202) 319–2460

Journal of Accountancy
American Institute of CPA's
330,000 circulation
(212) 575–6264

Journal of the American Dental Association
American Dental Association
140,000 circulation

Journal of the American Dietetic Association
The American Dietetic Association
65,000 circulation
(312) 899–0040

The Journal of Counseling & Development
American Association for Counseling & Development
60,000 circulation
(703) 823–9800

Journal of Petroleum Technology
Society of Petroleum Engineers
52,000 circulation
(214) 669–3377

Journal of Speech and Hearing Disorders
American Speech-Language-Hearing Association
73,000 circulation
(301) 897–0155

Junior League Review
Association of Junior Leagues International
187,000 circulation
(212) 683–1515

Life Association News
National Association of Life Underwriters
140,000 circulation
(202) 331-2179

Modern Maturity
American Association of Retired Persons
22 million
(212) 599-1880

National Guard
National Guard Association of the United States
70,000 circulation
(202) 789-0031

The National Voter
League of Women Voters
150,000 circulation
(202) 429-1965

Nature Conservancy
The Nature Conservancy
600,000 circulation
(703) 841-5300

The Northern Light
Supreme Council, Northern Masonic Jurisdiction
410,000 circulation
(617) 862-4410

Physical Therapy
American Physical Therapy Association
55,000 circulation
(703) 706-3180

Power Engineering
Institute of Electrical & Electronics Engineers, Inc.
50,000 circulation
(908) 562-3959

Real Estate Today
National Association of Realtors
785,000 circulation
(312) 329-8461

Realtor News
National Association of Realtors
760,000 circulation
(202) 383-1193

The Retired Officer Magazine
The Retired Officers Association
377,000 circulation
(703) 838-8105

School Food Service Journal
American Food Service Association
67,000 circulation
(703) 739-3900

The Sciences
The New York Academy of Sciences
70,000 circulation
(212) 838-0230

The Single Parent
Parents Without Partners, Inc.
120,000 circulation
(301) 588-9216

Social Work
National Association of Social Workers
140,000 circulation
(301) 565-0333

Tomorrow's Business Leader
Future Business Leaders of America
250,000 circulation
(703) 998-2534

Listing from *Who's Who SNAP Directory*. Used with permission of Society of National Association Publishers.

Appendix E

Top Association Trade Shows

Largest trade shows sponsored by associations, ranked by square feet of exhibition space needed.

Super Show–Sporting Goods Manufacturers Association–1,600,000

Radiological Society of North America Scientific Assembly and Annual Meeting–Radiological Society of North America–1,200,000

American International Toy Fair–Toy Manufacturers of America–1,000,000

Annual Experimental Aircraft Association International Convention and Sport Aviation–Experimental Aircraft Association–1,000,000

CONEXPO–Construction Industry Manufacturers Association–1,000,000

International Manufacturing Technology–Association for Manufacturers Technology–950,000

International Winter Consumer Electronics Show–Electronic Industries Association–837,068

PRINT–National Printing Equipment and Supply Association–807,000

National Housewares Manufacturers Association International Housewares Exhibition–National Housewares Manufacturers Association–800,000

NPE–National Plastics Exposition and Conference–Society of the Plastics Industry–800,000

International Lawn, Garden, and Power Equipment Exposition–Outdoor Power Equipment Association–770,990

Miami International Boat Show and Sailboat Show–National Marine Manufacturers Association–750,000

Midwest Manufactured Housing and Recreational Vehicle Show–Indiana Manufactured Housing Association–750,000

New Products Show–Sporting Goods Manufacturers Association–750,000

Northlands Farm and Ranch Show–Edmonton Northlands Association, Canada–723,000

North American International Auto Show–Detroit Auto Dealers Association–600,000

Southern California Boat Show–Southern California Marine Association–600,000

National Restaurant Association Restaurant Hotel-Motel Show–National Restaurant Association–575,023

American Psychiatric Association Annual Meeting–536,000

Recreation Vehicle Industry Association National RV Show–Recreation Vehicle Industry Association–536,000

Supermarket Industry Convention and Educational Exposition–Food Marketing Institute–520,000

Canadian Hardware Housewares and Home Improvement Show–Canadian Retail Hardware Association–500,000

Detroit Boat and Fishing Show–Michigan Boating Industries Association–500,000

National Association of Broadcasters International Convention and Exposition–National Association of Broadcasters–500,000

National Sporting Goods Association World Sports Exposition–National Sporting Goods Association–500,000

Ski Industries America Ski Show–United Ski Industries Association–500,000

United Ski Industries Association Ski Show and Sports Exposition–United Ski Industries Association–500,000

Appendix F

Association Prospecting Assistance

There are many associations that can provide corporations interested in marketing to associations with prospecting, marketing, and research assistance. Associations that represent association executives can provide corporations with avenues to reach their association members and often provide invaluable marketing and research assistance.

American Society of Association Executives
1575 Eye Street, N.W.
Washington, D.C. 20005
(202) 626–ASAE

ASAE Allied Societies

Alabama Council of Association Executives
400 South Union Street
Montgomery, AL 36104
(205) 262–8463

Society of Alaska Association Executives
c/o Southeast Alaska Tourism Council
P.O. Box 20710
Juneau, AK 99801
(907) 586–4777

Arizona Society of Association Executives
715 N. Third Street
Phoenix, AZ 85004
(602) 257–1185

Arkansas Society of Association Executives
P.O. Box 1556
Little Rock, AR 72203
(501) 376–2323

California Society of Association Executives
c/o Messersmith Group
1730 I Street #240
Sacramento, CA 95814
(916) 443–8980

Metro Los Angeles Association Executives
33 S. Catalina Ave. #202
Pasadena, CA 91106
(818) 449–4270

San Diego Society of Association Executives
1660 Hotel Circle North, Suite 604
San Diego, CA 92108
(619) 297–0453

San Francisco Bay Area Society of Association Executives
50 First Street #310
San Francisco, CA 94105
(415) 764–4942

Colorado Society of Association Executives
2170 S. Parker Rd. Suite 265
Denver, CO 80231
(303) 368–9090

Connecticut Society of Association Executives
71 East Avenue
Norwalk, CT 06851
(203) 852–7168

District of Columbia/Greater Washington Society of Association Executives
1426 21st Street N.W. #200
Washington, D.C. 20036
(202) 429–9370

Central Florida Society of Association Executives
c/o Kautter Management Group
P.O. Box 150127
Altomonte Springs, FL 32715
(407) 774–7880

Florida Society of Association Executives
1211 Semoran Blvd. #165
Casselberry, FL 32314
(407) 678–9344

South Florida Association Executives
c/o Promotrek, Inc.
P.O. Box 202
Boca Raton, FL 33429
(407) 391–3053

Tallahassee Society of Association Executives
c/o McCollum Management & Meetings
P.O. Box 10523
Tallahassee, FL 32302
(904) 222–7924

Georgia Society of Association Executives
c/o Professional Association Management
4500 Hugh Howell Rd. #140
Tucker, GA 30084
(404) 270–1248

Hawaii/Aloha Society of Association Executives
c/o Hemophilia Foundation
1100 Ward Avenue
Honolulu, HI 96814
(808) 521–5483

Idaho Society of Association Executives
P.O. Box 1664
Boise, ID 83701
(208) 343–1849

Chicago Society of Association Executives
20 N. Wacker Dr. #1456
Chicago, IL 60606
(312) 236–2288

Illinois Society of Association Executives
960 Clock Tower Drive, Suite J
Springfield, IL 62701
(217) 546–3006

Indiana Society of Association Executives
342 Mass. Ave. 200 Marott Center
Indianapolis, IN 46204
(317) 638–4402

Iowa Society of Association Executives
c/o Iowa Jewelers and Watchmakers Association
P.O. Box 22040
2175 NW 86th St. #14
Des Moines, IA 50322
(515) 270–1729

Kansas Society of Association Executives
4301 Huntoon Street, #9
Topeka, KS 66604
(913) 272–0083

Kentucky Society of Association Executives
c/o Association Professionals
1501 Twilight Trail
Frankfort, KY 40601
(502) 223–5322

Louisiana Society of Association Executives
c/o Norman Ferachi & Associates
603 Europe Street
Baton Rouge, LA 70802
(504) 387–3261

Maryland Society of Association Executives
c/o Joseph Shaner Co.
720 Light Street
Baltimore, MD 21230
(301) 752–3318

Michigan Society of Association Executives
1305 Abbott Road, Suite 105
East Lansing, MI 48823
(517) 336–4334

Southeast Michigan Society of Association Executives
2701 Troy Center Drive, Suite 125
Troy, MI 48207
(313) 362–9114

Mid-Michigan Society of Association Executives
1305 Abbott Road, Suite 105
East Lansing, MI 48823
(517) 366–4334

Minnesota Society of Association Executives
P.O. Box 7594
Minneapolis, MN 55407
(612) 729-7675

Mississippi Society of Association Executives
c/o Mississippi Association Managers
812 N. President St.
Jackson, MS 39211
(601) 354-2049

Kansas City Society of Association Executives
5818 Reeds Rd.
Mission, KS 66202
(913) 262-0163

Missouri Society of Association Executives
c/o Public Office Service
204 East High Street
Jefferson City, MO 65101
(314) 636-7521

St. Louis Society of Association Executives
25 Brentwood Blvd.
Clayton, MO 63105
(314) 721-2418

Montana Society of Association Executives
1825 Golden Avenue
Helena, MT 59601
(406) 442-5508

Nebraska Society of Association Executives
3120 O Street
Lincoln, NE 68510
(402) 476-1704

Nevada Society of Association Executives
c/o Las Vegas Board of REALTORS
300 S. Curry, Suite 3
Carson City, NV 89701
(702) 885-7200

New England Society of Association Executives
346-348 Washington St.
Braintree, MA 02184
(617) 848-9890

New Jersey Society of Association Executives
170 Township Line Road
Belle Mead, NJ 08502
(908) 359–1194

New Mexico Society of Association Executives
P.O. Box 27149
Albuquerque, NM 87125
(505) 292–0130

New York Society of Association Executives
322 8th Avenue, 12th Floor
New York, NY 10001
(212) 206–8230

Society of Association Executives of Upstate New York
275 1/2 Lark Street
Albany NY 12210
(518) 463–1755

North Carolina Association of Association Executives
P.O. Drawer 40399
Raleigh, NC 27629
(919) 790–8343

Cincinnati Society of Association Executives
c/o WJW Association Management
404 Bourbon Street
Blanchester, OH 45407
(513) 783–3870

Dayton Society of Association Executives
c/o Dayton Bar Association
1700 Hulman Building
Dayton, OH 45402
(513) 222–7902

Greater Cleveland Society of Association Executives
P.O. Box 26012
Cleveland, OH 44126
(216) 979–0211

Ohio Society of Association Executives
33 North High Street
Columbus, OH 43215
(614) 461–6026

Oklahoma Society of Association Executives
c/o Oklahomans For Energy and Jobs
120 North Robinson #3 West
Oklahoma City, OK 73102
(405) 236–8547

Tulsa Society of Association Executives
c/o Sweet Adelines International
5334 East 64th Street
Tulsa, OK 74147
(918) 622–1444

Oregon Society of Association Executives
825 NE 20th #120
Portland, OR 97232
(503) 236–9319

Delaware Valley Society of Association Executives
c/o Management Services, Inc.
P.O. Box 579
Moorestown, NJ 08057
(609) 234–0330

Harrisburg Trade Association Executives
c/o Pennsylvania Telephone Association
P.O. Box 1169
Harrisburg, PA 17108
(717) 238–8311

Pennsylvania Society of Association Executives
800 Corporate Circle #104
Harrisburg, PA 17110
(717) 545–1616

Pittsburgh Society of Association Executives
c/o Minerals, Metals, Materials Society
420 Commonwealth Drive
Warrendale, PA 15086
(412) 476–9035

Puerto Rico Society of Association Executives
c/o Puerto Rico Hotel and Tourism Association
Mirarmar Plaza, Stop 14
Santurce, PR 00907
(809) 725–2901

Rhode Island Conference of Association Executives
c/o Rhode Island Chamber of Commerce
400 Smith Street
Providence, RI 02908
(401) 272-1400

South Carolina Society of Association Executives
P.O. Box 11937
Columbia, SC 29211
(803) 771-4271

Memphis Society of Association Executives
c/o Southern Cotton Ginners Association
874 Cotton Gin Place
Memphis, TN 38106
(901) 974-3104

Tennessee Society of Association Executives
644 W. Iris Drive
Nashville, TN 37204
(615) 298-5944

Dallas/Fort Worth Association Executives
c/o International Furnishings and Design Association
107 World Trade Center
Dallas, TX 75220
(214) 747-2406

Houston Society of Association Executives
c/o Houston Chapter/American Institute of Architects
20 Greenway Plaza Suite 200
Houston, TX 77046
(713) 622-2081

San Antonio Society of Association Executives
c/o San Antonio Board of Realtors
9110 1H-10 West
San Antonio, TX 78230
(512) 593-1200

Texas Society of Association Executives
2550 South I-35 #200
Austin, TX 78704
(512) 444-1974

Utah Society of Association Executives
c/o Salt Lake Convention and Visitors Bureau
180 S. W. Temple
Salt Lake, UT 84101
(801) 521–2822

Vermont Society of Association Executives
c/o Vermont Trial Lawyers Association
P.O. Box 1562
Montpelier, VT 05601
(802) 223–0501

Virginia Society of Association Executives
c/o Easter Associates
620 Stagecoach Rd.
Charlottesville, VA 22901
(804) 977–3716

Washington Society of Association Executives
P.O. Box 473
Edmonds, WA 98020
(206) 778–6162

West Virginia Society of Association Executives
c/o Builders Supply Association of West Virginia
400 Allen Drive
Charleston, WV 25302
(304) 633–1966

Wisconsin Society of Association Executives
c/o Svinicki Association Services
1123 N. Water Street
Milwaukee, WI 53202
(414) 276–8788

ASAE International Affiliates   The ASAE also has affiliates located in Australia, Brazil, Canada, France, Dominican Republic, England, Switzerland, and the Philippines.

ADDITIONAL ASSOCIATION ASSISTANCE

Independent Sector
1828 L. Street, NW
Washington, D.C. 20036
(202) 223–8100

Institute of Association Management Companies
5700 Old Orchard Road, 1st Floor
Skokie, IL 60077
(708) 966–0880

International Exhibitors Association
5501 Baclick Rd. #200
Springfield, VA 22151
(703) 941–3725

National Council of Nonprofit Associations
1828 L Street, NW #505
Washington, D.C. 20036
(202) 785–3208

The Society for Nonprofit Organizations
6314 Odana Road, Suite 1
Madison, WI 53719
(800) 424–7367

Society of National Association Publications
1735 N. Lynn Street
Arlington, VA 22209
(703) 524–2000

Trade Show Bureau
1660 Lincoln Street, Suite 2080
Denver, CO 80264
(303) 860–7626

U.S. Chamber of Commerce
Association Department
1615 H Street, NW
Washington, D.C. 20062
(202) 463–5770

Appendix G

Prospecting Directories, Direct Mail, and Data Bases

DIRECTORIES

Associations Yellow Book
Monitor Publishing Company
104 Fifth Ave.
New York, NY 10011
(212) 627–4140

Encyclopedia of Associations
Gale Research, Inc.
835 Penobscot Bldg.
Detroit, MI 48226
(800) 877–GALE

Encyclopedia of Associations: International Organizations
Gale Research, Inc.
835 Penobscot Bldg.
Detroit, MI 48226
(800) 877–GALE

Encyclopedia of Associations: Regional, State and Local Organizations
Gale Research, Inc.
835 Penobscot Bldg.
Detroit, MI 48226
(800) 877–GALE

National Trade and Professional Associations of the U.S.
Columbia Books, Inc.
1212 New York Avenue, NW
Washington, D.C. 20077
(202) 898–0662

State and Regional Associations of the U.S.
Columbia Books, Inc.
1212 New York Avenue, NW
Washington, D.C. 20077
(202) 898–0662

Who's Who in Association Management
The American Society of Association Executives
1575 Eye Street, N.W.
Washington, D.C. 20005
(202) 626–2748

DIRECT MAIL LISTS

Direct Mail List Rates and Data

Standard Rate and Data
3004 Glenview Road
Wilmette, IL 60091
(708) 256–6067

American Society of Association Executives
Mailing List Rental
1575 Eye Street, N.W.
Washington, D.C. 20005
(202) 626–2711

Many of the directory publishers listed also sell or rent direct mail lists that are based on their directory data. In addition, many of the local associations of association executives also sell or rent mailing lists or directories of their association memberships. Refer to Appendix F for a listing of these associations.

DATA BASE ACCESS

DIALOG Information Retrieval Service: 800–3–DIALOG
The Encyclopedia of Associations Series available:
—National Associations of the U.S.
—International Associations
—Regional, State, and Local Associations

CD-ROM
GlobalAccess: Associations
The Encyclopedia of Associations Series is available

Books and Publications

Association Nondues Income: Balancing Purposes and Revenues
Order #-0074
U.S. Chamber of Commerce
1615 H Street, N.W.
Washington, D.C. 20062
(202) 463–5560

Association-Sponsored Insurance Programs (Catalog #121052)
ASAE-Informational Background Kit
1575 Eye Street, N.W.
Washington, D.C. 20005
(202) 626–2748

Association Insurance Program Guide & Survey Report
ASAE
1575 Eye Street, N.W.
Washington, D.C. 20005
(202) 626–2748

Marketing to Associations (Catalog #121024)
ASAE Publications
1575 Eye Street, N.W.
Washington, D.C. 20005
(202) 626–2748

Enterprise (For-Profit) Endeavors
Ed. Jill Muehrcke
The Society for Nonprofit Organizations
6314 Odana Rd. Suite #1
Madison, WI 53719
(608) 274–9777

Enterprise in the Nonprofit Sector, by James C. Crimmins and Mary
  Keil
Partners for Livable Places
1429 21st St.
Washington, D.C. 20036
(202) 887–5990

Exhibit Marketing (Catalog #210138)
ASAE Publications
1575 Eye Street, N.W.
Washington, D.C. 20005
(202) 626–2748

Filthy Rich and Other Nonprofit Fantasies, by Richard Steckel
Ten Speed Press © 1988
P.O. Box 7123
Berkeley, CA 94707
(415) 845–8414

Marketing The Nonprofit Association
The GWSAE Foundation
1426 21st. St. N.W. Suite 200
Washington, D.C. 20036
(202) 429–9370

Policies and Procedures in Association Management
Catalog #213016
American Society of Association Executives
1575 Eye Street, N.W.
Washington, D.C. 20005
(202) 626–2748

Selling to Associations: Advice from Association Executives
ASAE Information Central White Paper
The American Society of Association Executives
1575 Eye Street, N.W.
Washington, D.C. 20005
(202) 626–2748

Something Ventured, Something Gained, by Laura Landy
ACA Books
American Council for the Arts
1285 Avenue of the Americas
New York, NY 10019
(212) 223–2787

Sources of Nondues Income
ASAS Information Background Kit
1575 Eye Street, N.W.
Washington, D.C. 20005
(202) 626–2748

Strategic Marketing, by David Cravens
Richard D. Irwin, Inc. © 1982
1333 Burr Ridge Parkway
Burr Ridge, IL 60521

Study of Cause-Related Marketing
By Sheridan Associates & Zimmerman Associates
Independent Sector
1828 L Street N.W.
Washington, D.C. 20036
(202) 223–8100

The Third America, by Michael O'Neil
Jossey-Bass © 1989
350 Samson Street
San Francisco, CA 94104
(415) 433–1767

Index